THE GREEK ISLANDS
Genius Loci

View of Naxos island seen through the monumental doorway of the Archaic temple.
Thomas Hope (1769-1831)   Watercolour, 44 x 29 cm.   Benaki Museum, Inv. No. 27375.

Author's acknowledgements

This series of twenty books covering the Aegean Islands is the fruit of many years of solitary dedication to a job difficult to accomplish given the extent of the subject matter and the geography involved. My belief throughout has been that only what is seen with the eyes can trustfully be written about; and to that end I have attempted to walk, ride, drive, climb, sail and swim these Islands in order to inspect everything talked about here. There will be errors in this text inevitably for which, although working in good faith, I alone am responsible. Notwithstanding, I am confident that these are the best, most clearly explanatory and most comprehensive artistic accounts currently available of this vibrant and historically dense corner of the Mediterranean.

Professor Robin Barber, author of the last, general, *Blue Guide to Greece* (based in turn on Stuart Rossiter's masterful text of the 1960s), has been very generous with support and help; and I am also particularly indebted to Charles Arnold for meticulously researched factual data on the Islands and for his support throughout this project. For generously sharing his knowledge of Aghios Efstratios with me for this volume, I am especially grateful to Vyron Manikakis. I could not have asked for a more saintly and helpful editor, corrector and indexer than Judy Tither. Efi Stathopoulou, Peter Cocconi, Marc René de Montalembert, Valentina Ivancich, William Forrester and Geoffrey Cox have all given invaluable help; and I owe a large debt of gratitude to John and Jay Rendall for serial hospitality and encouragement. For companionship on many journeys, I would like to thank a number of dear friends: Graziella Seferiades, Ivan Tabares, Matthew Kidd, Martin Leon, my group of Louisianan friends, and my brother Iain— all of whose different reactions to and passions for Greece have been a constant inspiration.

This work is dedicated with admiration and deep affection to Ivan de Jesus Tabares-Valencia who, though a native of the distant Andes mountains, from the start understood the profound spiritual appeal of the Aegean world.

McGILCHRIST'S GREEK ISLANDS

12. LEMNOS
WITH AGHIOS EFSTRATIOS & SAMOTHRACE

GENIUS LOCI PUBLICATIONS
London

McGilchrist's Greek Islands 12 Lemnos with Aghios Efstratios &
Samothrace
First edition

Published by Genius Loci Publications
54 Eccleston Road, London W13 0RL

Nigel McGilchrist © 2010
Nigel McGilchrist has asserted his moral rights.

ISBN 978-1-907859-17-5

A CIP catalogue record of this book is available from the British Library.

The author and publisher cannot accept responsibility or liability for
information contained herein, this being in some cases difficult to verify
and subject to change.

Layout and copy-editing by Judy Tither

Cover design by Kate Buckle

Maps and plans by Nick Hill Design

Printed and bound in Great Britain by TJ International Ltd, Padstow, Cornwall

The island maps in this series are based on the cartography of
Terrain Maps
Karneadou 4, 106 75 Athens, Greece
T: +30 210 609 5759, Fx: +30 210 609 5859
terrain@terrainmaps.gr
www.terrainmaps.gr

This book is one of twenty which comprise the complete, detailed
manuscript which the author prepared for the *Blue Guide: Greece,
the Aegean Islands* (2010), and on which the *Blue Guide* was
based. Some of this text therefore appears in the *Blue Guide*.

A NOTE ON THE TEXT & MAPS

Some items in the text are marked with an asterisk: these may be monuments, landscapes, curiosities or individual artefacts and works of art. The asterisk is not simply an indication of the renown of a particular place or item, but is intended to draw the reader's attention to things that have a uniquely interesting quality or are of particular beauty.

A small number of hotels and eateries are also marked with asterisks in the *Practical Information* sections, implying that their quality or their setting is notably special. These books do not set out to be guides to lodging and eating in the Islands, and our recommendations here are just an attempt to help with a few suggestions for places that have been selected with an eye to simplicity and unpretentiousness. We believe they may be the kind of places that a reader of this book would be seeking and would enjoy.

On the island maps:

⁂   denotes a site with visible prehistoric or ancient remains

☦   denotes a church referred to in the text
(on Island Maps only rural churches are marked)

✝   denotes a monastery, convent or large church referred to in the text

⌘   denotes a Byzantine or Mediaeval castle

♟   denotes an ancient stone tower

♨   denotes an important fresh-water or geothermic spring

⛴   denotes a harbour with connecting ferry services

Road and path networks:

- a continuous line denotes a metalled road
or unsurfaced track feasible for motors

- a dotted line denotes footpath only

CONTENTS

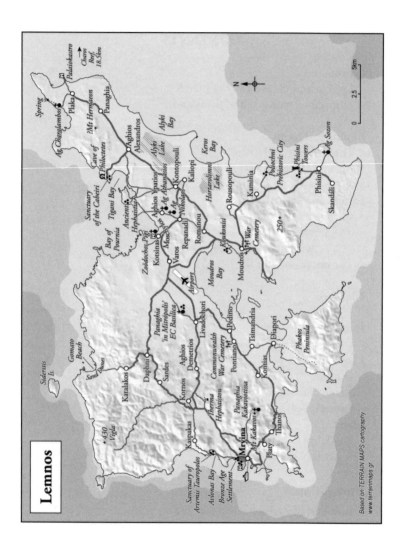

Lemnos

Based on TERRAIN MAPS cartography
www.terrainmaps.gr

LEMNOS

Lemnos has some of the most unusual landscapes of the northern Aegean islands—not only its mountainous west but also the grassy, rolling expanses of the east have a character not encountered elsewhere. The west is rugged and Aegean; while the east is more Anatolian in feel. The whole island is volcanic in nature and displays much of the geophysical torment of its formation. A reef, some way out to sea from its eastern shore may even be an island mentioned by both Homer and Sophocles which, according to Pausanias, had by his time disappeared under water in an earthquake. Given its appearance, it comes as no surprise that Lemnos was always held sacred to Hephaestus (Vulcan), the god of fire and of the forge—a fascinating divinity, born without the physical perfection of the other gods, and who was hurled down onto Lemnos from Mount Olympus during a dispute between his mother, Hera, and Zeus (*Iliad*, I. 590). Hephaestus remains the hard-working and artful outsider of the Olympian pantheon; but his cult on Lemnos at Hephaistia and his association with the sanctuary of the Cabeiri (whose father he was, according to Herodotus) substantially pre-dates Greek settlement on the island. Lemnos, with its once ac-

tive volcanic fumaroles and its position on the routes to
and from the mines and ore-deposits of the Black Sea and
Anatolia, was well positioned to be one of the earliest centres of metal-working in the Aegean. As a result the island
acquired importance very early on in prehistoric times. In
1930 what is generally considered to be the oldest organised city in Europe was uncovered by Italian archaeologists at Poliochni, on the island's east coast. And the links
with Italian archaeology continue through the important
'Lemnos *stele*'—a late 6th century BC inscription in the
native Lemnian language, which bears extraordinary affinities with the Etruscan language and which has altered
scholarly thinking on the question of the origins of the
Etruscans. The *stele* is now in Athens.

The villages and towns of Lemnos are sober, but not
without the charm of an attractive local style of architecture. A combination of less convenient connections
and a big military presence has slowed the growth of
tourism on the island and left it out of the main stream
of development. This is its charm. A quiet and not in-
elegant main town, Myrina, dominated by an impressive Venetian castle; remarkable prehistoric remains; the
panoramic cave-church of the Panaghía Kakaviótissa; the
remote and beautiful beach of Gomati; therapeutic, geothermic springs; a scattering of delightful villages; peace,

quiet and a rich flora and birdlife—all make Lemnos a memorable place to stay. An added pleasure to a visit is the island's fragrant wine.

LEGEND & HISTORY

The legends and mythology associated with Lemnos are particularly rich and important, and explain the complexity of the island's history. From Naxos, Dionysos brought Ariadne to Lemnos, where she gave birth to his sons, among them, Thoas. Not long after, Aphrodite punished the womenfolk of Lemnos—because they had purportedly impugned her virtue—with a lingering, unsavoury odour which prevented the men of the island from having intercourse with them. The men took Thracian concubines from the mainland instead. The women of Lemnos thereupon took revenge by murdering all the island's menfolk except for Thoas, now their king, who escaped through the compassion of his daughter, Hypsipyle. A year or so later when Jason and the Argonauts put in at Myrina on their voyage to Colchis the women feared a counter-attack; but on the advice of an old woman, they received the men with hospitality, sleeping with them so as to ensure the continuity of their tribe. Hypsipyle bore Jason twin sons, before he departed again for Colchis on his mission to find the Golden Fleece. Diodorus Siculus (*Bibliotheke*, III.55 ff) furthermore says that Myrina, the queen of the warlike, female tribe of Amazons from North

Africa, on her campaigns conquering lands in the Eastern Mediterranean, founded many cities. Amongst them was 'one which bore her own name' (there is another ancient Myrina on the coast of Asia Minor, north of Smyrna, in addition to the one on Lemnos); she also founded a city on Lesbos 'named Mytilene, after her sister'. Women are of primary importance throughout the story of Lemnos and its neighbouring islands. An interesting epilogue is provided by another literary tradition. It was Hercules in the end who destroyed the Amazons. On his death he bequeathed his bow and arrows to the archer Philoctetes with the request that he be the person to light his pyre. Philoctetes, who was among the Greek heroes who sailed to Troy, was bitten by a snake during a stop on the journey, and the ensuing wound became gangrenous and began to smell so badly that Odysseus, on the orders of Agamemnon, abandoned him on Lemnos or on nearby Chryse (*see below, pp. 50–52*). Cured eventually of his affliction, he was later brought back to the Greek camp at Troy and was the warrior who was later to kill Paris. Lemnos—which in earlier days of volcanic activity may well have been a place of bad, sulphurous odours—produced a kind of sacred, medicinal clay of volcanic origin, known throughout history as 'Lemnian Earth' (*see below, pp. 39–41*) which was widely used for the curing of snake-bites. The dense and suggestive weave of themes, recurrences and cross-references in this combination of myth, history and geography is perhaps the richest of any among the many islands' stories.

Exploits of the sexes appear once again in the fore in a story from historic times which gave rise according to Herodotus (*Hist.* VI, 138) to the expression 'Lemnian deeds', meaning 'atrocities'. During the Persian Wars the Lemnians, in an act of revenge, carried off Athenian women from the Sanctuary of Artemis at Brauron in Attica and took them back to be concubines in Lemnos. The resulting children borne by the women soon began to look down on their local half-brothers—whereupon the Lemnians slaughtered both the upstart children and their Athenian mothers. Crops failed thereafter on the island. When in desperation the islanders consulted the Delphic Oracle, its recommendations led eventually to the island's submission to the Athenian yoke.

Homer mentions that the people of Lemnos were the ('wild-voiced') Sintians; Herodotus and Thucydides mention that they were Pelasgians or Tyrrhenians, indicating perhaps different stages of pre-Greek history. Whatever their identity, they were not of Greek stock in earliest times and had come to the island from the Thracian or Anatolian mainlands: the earliest Greek inscription from the island is dated to c. 500 BC.

Archaeology has shown that Lemnos had an advanced Neolithic civilisation and a Bronze Age culture of Minoan-Mycenaean type, connected with Troy and Lesbos, which continued without a sharp break into the Geometric period. The island fell to Persia in 513 BC and changed hands more than once before the end of the Persian wars. Hippias is said to have died here after Marathon. From 477 BC the island formed part of the Delian League, paying an annual tribute of nine talents; it later had a clerurchy imposed by Athens. It was these clerurchs who dedicated the famous Lemnian *Athena* of Pheidias on the Athenian Acropolis. Lemnian troops fought for Athens at Sphacteria (425 BC), at Amphipolis (422 BC) and at Syracuse (413 BC). Apart from brief periods of domination by Sparta (404–393 BC), by the Macedonians, and by Antiochus the Great, Lemnos remained principally under Athenian influence, and was one of her advance bases in the northern Aegean, along with Imbros and Skyros: although the immediate governance may have been Athenian, ultimate control was latterly exercised by Rome, until independence for the island was granted by Septimius Severus. Both Theophrastus in the 4th century BC and Galen in the 2nd century AD visited and were interested in the properties of the island's renowned 'Lemnian earth'

The island was plundered by the Germanic tribe of the Heruli in the late 3rd century AD, and later passed under Byzantine rule. In 325 a bishop, Strategios, of Lemnos was present at the 1st Council of Nicaea, and the island was raised to a metropolitan see under Leo VI (886–912). In 924 the Saracen fleet under Leo of Tripoli was defeated by a Byzantine naval force in the waters off Lemnos. In 1136 the Venetians officially obtained their first foothold on the island at Kotsinas, and from 1207 Lemnos became the fief of the Venetian, Navigajoso family. In the 13th to 15th centuries the island was disputed between Venice, Genoa and Byzantium—the subsequent, brief Genoese rule from 1453–55 being so harsh that the inhabitants pled with Sultan Mehmet II to liberate and rule them instead. A papal force landed, however, the following year as part of a crusade under Callixtus III to repossess Constantinople. A new religious order of Knights was founded on the island, along the lines of the Knight Hospitallers of St

John, by Pius II; but Lemnos finally fell, following a series of disputes with the Venetians, to the Ottoman Sultanate in 1479 which later used it as a place of exile for disgraced notables. Count Orloff's Russian force occupied the island in the war of 1770, but was driven out by the Ottoman naval commander, Hassan Bey. For a few months in 1829 Lemnos became part of free Greece before being given back to Turkey in exchange for Euboea. In 1912 the island was liberated by the Greek admiral, Koundouriotis. The Gulf of Moudros was the base in 1915 for the disastrous Dardanelles expedition. Under the terms of the Treaties of Sèvres (1920) and of Lausanne (1923), Lemnos became an internationally recognised part of the Greek State.

The guide to the island has been divided into two sections:
- *Myrina and the west of the island*
- *Moudros and the east of the island*

MYRINA & THE WEST OF THE ISLAND

MYRINA

The appearance of the island from the sea before arriving at the principal town and harbour of Mýrina leaves no doubt as to its volcanic origins. The empty mountains of its west coast seem more dramatic than their modest height merits because they possess the torn and rugged forms of recent volcanic formation. **Mýrina** itself is situated between two fine bays, and hides behind the massive bulwark of a rock peninsular on its seaward side, crowned by the impressive curtain walls of its castle. The town is small, lively, and architecturally dignified. There is a pleasing mixture of Ottoman and Neoclassical buildings—some Thracian-style timbered houses with *sachnisia* (projecting upper floors with wooden frames) and a preponderance of stone mansions of the period from 1880 to 1930 with symmetrical façades comprising stone window- and door-frames and decorative entablatures, especially along the sweep of Roméikos Beach to the north.

At the beginning of the long curving main street (Kyda Street) of the old quarter of Myrina, which begins at the corner of the inner harbour, are two vestiges from the Ottoman past: at the end of an alleyway just north of the *Hotel Aktaion* is an abandoned octagonal, 18th century **türbe** or mausoleum, and at the corner of the first block on Kyda Street is a **fountain** of excellent spring water, still bearing its original Osmanli inscription of 1771 carved in white marble and framed by the local, magenta-grey volcanic stone.

From the corner of the harbour, Themistokleous and Nefelis Streets lead up to a panoramic saddle below the **castle** which occupies a natural fortress of rock to the west. (*Unrestricted access.*) As you climb up, the massive irregular stone blocks of the **Archaic acropolis walls** (6th century BC) are visible high up to the left amongst the volcanic folds and protrusions of the rock; they appear again at the highest level of the north face underneath the later, Venetian walls. The impregnability and visibility of the site has been appreciated since early antiquity. Rock-cut channels can be seen in the vicinity of these early fortifications for ducting and collecting rain water. Although the inner fortress on the summit was probably erected over Byzantine foundations by the Venetians in the early 13th century, the majority of the fortifications visible today were built by the Genoese and Venetians in the 15th century, and later modified and added to by the

Turks (especially on the north side and in the eastern artillery emplacements). In 1273 the forces of the Byzantine Emperor Michael VIII Palaiologos took three years to besiege and capture the castle from the Venetian Navigajoso overlords. Today, wild deer are permitted to graze in the interior, giving life to an otherwise abandoned area.

In the middle of the rough path leading up to the gateway of the Venetian enceinte is a finely-turned, ancient column base in Thasian marble. Entrance to the fortress is through **three successive gates** with monolithic door-posts, set in a treacherous defile between walls; between the first and last gate an intruder was effectively trapped in a blind, zig-zag chasm of walls. The two roofless buildings ahead as you emerge from the gates are Ottoman constructions: the **administrative building** and barracks to the right and, slightly above it, the **mosque**. Stairs for the minaret can be seen on the north side of the latter, and the indented *mihrab* (which does not protrude externally like a Christian apse) in its southeast wall.

To the south side, the castle avails itself of a deep, natural, rock ditch for protection, while on the gentler north slope there are three—and, in places, four—curtain walls, the lowest (Ottoman) fortifications being almost at the level of the shore. At the highest point of the enclosed area is the **inner keep**; near where a couple of pieces of ancient marble have been immured, there are signs that the natural rock has been cut into a terrace in Antiquity. This could possibly relate to one of the two sanctuaries of Artemis attested in inscriptions—the one referred to as 'in Myrina'.

A further area of interest lies on the lower western face of the hill, where there is a complex of storage buildings for water and supplies. The large **roofed cistern building** here in a walled enclosure is probably of Venetian origin, but substantially reworked in Ottoman times. The slight *talus* of the walls for reinforcement below the external string-course of the cistern house and the proliferation of vegetation within the enclosure confirm its use for water storage. Inside, a small antechamber precedes the main interior where the pool in the floor, now filled in, is surrounded by a rectangular border of flagstones. The large **vaulted magazines** to the side are structures raised by the Venetians; the flight of steps—a couple of which are faced with inscribed Ottoman gravestones laid flat—cut into the rock date from the Second World War and lead into an underground gallery enlarged in the same period. Directly below at the shore in the northwestern corner, a natural cleft in the rocks has created a small, **hidden 'harbour'** with space for one boat: the sides of the rock-face show roughly cut loop-holes for the mooring ropes.

Archaeological Museum

(*Open daily 8.30–3, except Mon.*) This interesting and unusual collection is displayed over two floors of a small neoclassical mansion, formerly the Ottoman Governor's offices, in the middle of the north shore of Myrina.

The *lower floor* is devoted to: first, prehistoric Poliochni and Myrina (entrance vestibule and rooms to either side); and second, a collection of funerary art and inscriptions (rear of the building). Throughout the prehistoric collections, and at the sites themselves on the island, chronological periods have been designated colours for the sake of clarity, as follows:

Black	3500–3100 BC	—(*predating metalwork*)
Blue	3100–2750 BC	
Green	2750–2500 BC	
Red	2500–2300 BC	—(*pottery of the red is*
Yellow	2300–2000 BC	*distinguished from green*
Brown	2000–1500 BC	*by a greater and more*
Violet	1500–1200 BC	*complex variety of*
		plastic forms)

Some of the most striking and beautiful pottery designs, as yet undecorated, already make their appearance in the mid 4th millennium BC ('Black' period), such as the beautifully proportioned **shallow cup with large loop handles** (in ∞ form), and the graceful, **high-stemmed 'fruit-stands'**—a striking design which persisted into later epochs (*see nos.14 & 15 in hallway*). A lighter, burnished surface, sometimes decorated with incisions and knobs, nipples or handles for hanging, appears in the 'Blue' period; cooking pots and strainer vases, perhaps for cheese making, also evolve and are perfected in the later 'Red' period. The most distinctive design of all perhaps appears in the 'Yellow' period (*Room 2, to right*)—the remarkably refined and elongated, *****two-handled chalices** from Poliochni (*nos. 27 & 28*). Some of the finely wrought **gold artefacts** found in room 643 at Poliochni are displayed here; the remainder of what was found is now displayed in the National Archaeological Museum in Athens.

The epigraphic collection (*rear area*) contains a wide variety of types of inscription and qualities of lettering. Note the large number of **boundary stones** used for the demarcation of private land, which often contain information on whether the plot in question has been mortgaged against a loan ('*ΠΕΠΡΑΜΕΝΟΝ ΕΠΙ ΛΥΣΕΙ*'). Several of the *stelai* are honorific in nature and bear lightly incised wreaths at the top; the funerary inscriptions are shorter—the name, patronym and deme of the deceased, followed by the simple salutation '*XAIPE*', 'bids farewell': a decree of Dimitros of Phaleron, Governor of Athens, also in the collection, specifically restricts the opulence of grave *stelai*. Another group of inscriptions relates to the manumission of slaves by their owners, a frequent occurrence which regularly coincided with ceremonies at the sanctuary of the Cabeiri. Amongst the sculpture exhibited, of particular note is the headless **statue of Eros**—a good Roman copy of an original bronze by Lysippus of the 4th century BC.

The *upper floor* contains smaller items, from the 8th century BC through to Roman times, except for the one room of **metalwork** which exhibits pieces deriving from all periods of the island's history, stretching all the way from finds at Poliochni ('Blue' and 'Red' periods)—bone-handled awls, hooks, spindles and metalworking tools—through gold and bronze jewellery and a set of exquisitely formed bronze handles and statuette fragments of the Hellenistic period, down to coins of the Byzantine era. On the main landing (*rear wall*) are finds from Hellenistic ceramic workshops on the island (note especially the beautiful slip-painted ivy design on the two-handled cup, *no. 8*), including several intricate moulds for the mass-production of items which are nonetheless of the highest quality. The most striking exhibits are in the right-hand corner room—a magnificent collection of *terracotta figures of Sirens** of the 7th & 6th centuries BC from the sanctuary of the Great Goddess at Hephaistia: their wide-eyed expressions gave them apotropaic powers. Note also here the **Cybele figurine** (*no. 111*) with drum in her left hand and lion cub in her lap, and the series of (once decorated) votive terracotta plaques of musicians, and statuettes of citharodes. The central room exhibits, exactly as it was found, the **burial of a sacrificial bullock** from the sanctuary of Artemis *Tauropolos* at Avlonas, and a collection of large, vigorously painted '*dinos*' kraters, reassembled from fragments.

In the front left room the elegance of the **Archaic *kantharoi*** (drinking cups) with slender arching handles (*nos. 24, 25 & 27*) seems to echo the refinement and simplicity of their prehistoric precursors on the floor below.

In the area of *garden* at the front of the museum are the larger stone pieces—conspicuous among them a block, later carved with a cross and re-used in Early Christian times, inscribed with a **decree** of the 'Boule of the Athenians of Hephaistia'—showing how the settling clerurchs from Athens reconstituted the same governmental practices of their home city while colonising Lemnos and never lost their identity as Athenians in the process.

On the other side of the shoreline road from the museum
is a white marble monument to the memory of the Russian naval commanders, Count Alexei Orloff and Dimitry
Seniavin, whose squadrons called at Lemnos during the
Russian-Turkish wars of 1770 and 1807, giving support
during the struggles against Ottoman dominion. Two
hundred metres further north along the shore, opposite
and inland of the promontory (now occupied by the Officers' Club building) which separates the 'Roméikos' and
'Richá Nerá' beaches is a large area of recent and well-
documented excavations revealing the site of **Prehistoric
Myrina**.

Although evidence is coming to light of other, smaller prehistoric settlements on the island, Poliochni in the East and
Myrina in the west are the two principal poles of habitation in Bronze Age Lemnos. Both are exceptionally early,
large-scale, proto-urban settlements which evolved con-
temporaneously. By comparison with Poliochni, Myrina has
yielded markedly less from the 4th and early 3rd millennia
BC ('Black' & 'Blue' periods), but appears to have flourished
more extensively and become a larger settlement in the late
3rd millennium BC ('Red' & 'Yellow' periods), with larger
and marginally more sophisticated building designs. A large
area has been uncovered and painstakingly consolidated

by the archaeologists revealing the stone foundations of a closely packed conurbation of houses, organised in (kinship) groups and neighbourhoods.

What is immediately striking is the multitude of different colours of stones used which, given that the walls may not have been rendered, would have imparted life and distinction to them. The spaces between houses were narrow, although endowed with the elements for drainage. The houses themselves were roofed with seaweed packed with mud over wooden rafters; a few may have had improvised storage lofts (*House B*). Some of the houses are 'semi-detached', with a single construction comprising several dwellings with separated entrances. The intercommunicating, windowless rooms of the interior appear to have been surprisingly uncramped.

Although two large areas have been excavated they represent only a small part of the whole settlement which would have begun on the raised promontory now occupied by the Officers' Club and subsequently spread down into the surrounding area. The houses appear to have been shaken down by earthquakes more than once and rebuilt over the ruins of the previous phase.

Panaghía Kakaviótissa

The southwest corner of the island is dominated inland by the jagged peaks of Mount Kákavos (280m) which rise 4km to the east of Myrina. Inside the eyebrow of a wide cave just below the summit is tucked the whitewashed structure of the chapel of the **Panaghía Kakaviótissa**— object of an important *panegyri* and procession on the first Tuesday after Easter. A monastic community is first recorded here in the early 14th century when it was a dependence of the Great Lavra Monastery on Mount Athos; hermitic presence and cult on this spot, however, goes back far earlier. In the rocky landscape around are many artificial cavities and niches, and at the summit is a rock-cut terrace of presumably very ancient cultic use: the panoramic views from it are such as to evoke a spiritual joy. (*The cave is reached in one and a half hours by foot from Myrina, preferably by taking the driveable track which heads due east from the Platý/Kornós road 1.1km north of the main road junction north of Platý, and following the steep path and steps which make the final approach from the northwest.*)

THE WEST OF THE ISLAND:
SOUTH LOOP VIA KONTIAS &
LIVADOCHORI

The southwest corner of Lemnos is a treeless landscape of volcanic boulders, with alternating shoreline plains, sandy bays and needle-like outcrops of rock. There has been some extensive building in recent years, but the old, hidden centres of both **Platý** (1.4km) and **Thános** (3.5km) are composed of stone houses in attractive vernacular architecture and small squares with pergola-shaded tavernas. The greatest interest and variety is in the beautiful village of *****Kontiás** (10km), which lies in the dip between two volcanic outcrops—that to the north fringed with a forest of pines and cypress, that to the south crowned by the chapel of Aghios Athanasios, and carpeted on its lower north and west sides by a remarkably prolific lichen of a rich yellow/orange colour. The varied forms, colours and textures of the symmetrically cuboid houses, the irregular volcanic boulders and the dark trees have all the elements of a Provençal composition by Cézanne. At the centre of the village is the stately 19th century church of Aghios Demetrios, fronted by a wide porch with carved capitals. To its south, the balconied façade of a former shop built in the 1930s sports a decoratively moulded entablature, typical of the attention to whimsical detail in local Lemnian architecture.

At the south end of the village are several abandoned windmills; from this area a road leads southeast to Diapóri (13km) on the isthmus of the **Phakós peninsula**—a tree-less, softly folded, protrusion of hilly land given over to sheep-raising and pasture, and a natural and undisturbed **wild-life preserve**. The skies are full of larks and wheel-ing rock-doves; Hobby, Peregrine falcon and Eleonora's falcon, with their characteristically hook-winged profile, hunt in the air above. Hugging the ground, the Chukar partridge, with its banded flanks, can sometimes be seen. Occasional efflorescences of coloured rock—white, yel-low and red—break the surface of the land where there were once fumaroles and vapour holes which are now extinct. The only buildings to be seen are the traditional, **stone-built stock-barns** which cling to the contours of the ground—simple, functional structures with a long and unchanging architectural ancestry.

At the hills of Vrío Kastro to the south, and Troch-aliá to the east of Tsimándria, finds from the Bronze Age have been made; the sites have restricted access, however, because of the military presence. At **Portianó** (14km), northwest of the village centre (along 'Anzac Street') be-hind the local Orthodox cemetery-church, is the **Com-**

monwealth War Cemetery where a small portion of the total British and Anzac soldiers who died on the ill-fated Gallipoli expedition in April and May of 1915 are buried.

The Dardanelles and Gallipoli Campaign was launched in an attempt to capture Istanbul and to force Turkey out of the war. After disheartening loss of life, the Dardanelles area was evacuated by the Allies in December and January of 1915/16. The large, protected inlet of Moudros Bay to the east of here was the principal base for the operations. At the end of the war, the armistice between Turkey and the Allied Forces was signed on 30th October 1918 aboard HMS *Agamemnon* in Moudros Bay. Three Egyptian labourers and an Ottoman Commander are also buried in the cemetery.

After passing through Pedinó (15.5km), many of whose traditional houses were badly affected by an earthquake in 1968, the route joins the main Myrina/airport road at Livadochóri (20km). By crossing over the airport highway, and taking the road northeast along the east side of the army camp from the traffic lights just after the *Gymnásio* (school), you reach after 2km the remarkable church of the **Panaghia in Mitropolis** (*not signed*). (*The track drops down to some farm buildings in a hollow after the asphalt finishes; the church is inside the farm-yard,* *which is not kept closed.*) The present chapel is a modern construction, but sits on and among a mass of *spolia* from an **Early Christian basilica**—possibly in turn built over the base of a pagan temple. Two monolithic columns of Proconnesian marble stand in the porch: another lies on the ground to the southwest, beside two enormous **sarcophagi**—one beautifully decorated with crosses and rosettes in roundels—now commandeered as water-troughs for animals. The confident quality of the carving suggests an early date, possibly 5th century AD, though some commentators (Hetherington: *The Greek Islands—Byzantine and Mediaeval Buildings*, 2001) have given the work an 11th century date. Over the entrance door of the church is a marble beam with an 11th century inscription and an immured Byzantine Ionic-style capital. The floor inside is laid with marble fragments of an Early Byzantine *templon*. In the centre of the apse is a simple, stone, episcopal throne. It is this seat of a bishop which explains the church's epithet 'in Mitropolis'. It is hard to date the massive podium blocks underpinning the north side of the church which may have been adapted from a pre-existing pagan structure on the site to form the base of the Early Christian basilica.

By the direct route west, Livadochóri is 15km from Myrina. The main road rises to Aghios Dimítrios, centre of production of Lemnos's distinctive and fragrant wine. As the road descends again, a branch road from the junction 6km from Myrina and 11km from Livadochóri, leads 1km east to **Thérma Hephaístou**, the island's principal geothermic springs. Beside the road, about 500m before arriving at Therma, is a small cold spring of mineral water; in the area just above the main bath-complex a freestanding fountain, re-designed in 1908 and bearing an inscription to that effect in both Osmanli and Greek, gushes a prized hot water, avidly collected by locals in jars for its remarkable digestive and curative properties. To the west of it is the former thermal establishment, now abandoned. Below, is the new one which is organised as a sleek hydrotherapy spa (*www.thermaspa.gr—open 11–10*) offering a variety of massages and immersions in water pools at 42–45°C.

THE WEST OF THE ISLAND:
NORTH LOOP VIA KASPAKAS & DAPHNI

The extension of the road north from Myrina along Roméikos and Richá Nerá bays, crosses a small promontory and drops down to the estuarial bay of Avlónas—once the marshy and reedy harbour for what appears to have been a **sanctuary of Artemis** (2.5km)—worshipped here possibly as 'Artemis *Tauropolos*', given the figurines of oxen and the skeleton of a sacrificial bull found at the site. The excavated remains of the sanctuary are somewhat improbably to be found right in the middle of a luxury hotel complex (*Hotel Porto Myrina*) surrounded by holiday villas. The site was only discovered and documented in the process of building the hotel.

A comprehensive view of the remaining visible area can had from the upper floor of the hotel's lobby, although there is no material to help the visitor understand the complex site: indeed its layout is still little understood by archaeologists. There are several construction phases: (1) a central core of 7th/6th century BC buildings (two overlying apsidal buildings with ancillary rooms); (2) a principally Hellenistic overlay of more rectangular spaces (perimeter walls, and rooms looking onto an open space in the centre of the precinct); and (3) small amounts of Roman construction at the southern extremity.

A long rectangular room with stone benches at the north-west end of the inner enclosure may have functioned as an assembly room during initiation rituals. Door-posts and thresholds, and some large areas of paving of the open spaces are generally well-preserved. As elsewhere on the island, at Hephaistia and at the sanctuary of the Cabeiri, the typology of the early sacred buildings here is not that of the standard Greek sanctuary organised around a temple and altar: it is of an oriental, pre-Greek model based on the telesterion-type of building, generally associated with mystery cults (*see under sanctuary of the Cabeiri, pp. 45–49*).

From Avlonas the road rises swiftly to **Káspakas** (5.5km), a village of traditional houses and narrow streets, sited precariously above a steep and fertile valley. At the road junction (10km) north of Kórnos a branch road leads left into the mountainous and rugged, northwest corner of the island towards the island's highest summit of Vigla (430m). The road is arduous but rewarding for the beauty of its panoramic and untamed landscapes. (*This is a military zone and the furthest sectors of the road and adjacent areas may be rendered out of bounds by military manoeuvres.*) The main road continues to Sardés (12.5km),

Dáphni (16km), and lastly to Katálakos (19km) which lies almost hidden from sight in a ravine: these are attractive and unvisited villages, where unaffected, traditional foods and the island's fragrant wine can be sampled. In the village of **Sardés**, a working blacksmith's shop survives—one of the last in a millennial tradition on Lemnos. At Katálakos the asphalt ends and a steep track leads a further 4km down to **Gomáti Beach**, one of the island's most beautiful bays, backed by high, sweeping sand-dunes.

From the junction at Daphni the road descends in 8km to the main highway at the airport, just west of the isthmus of the island.

MOUDROS &
THE EAST OF THE ISLAND

(*20km east of Myrina by the most direct route, is the road junction at Varos. The itinerary below follows first the north branch from the junction to Pláka, and then the south branch to Skandáli. Distances are measured from the junction.*)

NORTH BRANCH

At **Kótsinas** (3km) (formerly known as 'Kokkinos') a mound-like promontory projects into the bay of Pourniá. Buried in it and visible partially at the western side and along the shoreline are the ruins of a once important Byzantine /Venetian castle.

In 1136, Michael, Archbishop of Lemnos ceded the site to Venetian merchants: within 70 years the Venetians had become overlords of Lemnos, with the installing of the Navigajoso dynasty of rulers. A pre-existing Byzantine fortress must have been built up into a castle by the Venetians in 1397 when this became their garrison headquarters. The (partially) sheltered bay was the roadstead for their ships: the submerged remains of a jetty are still visible. The last

Emperor of Byzantium, Constantine XI Dragases, was be-
sieged here, together with his second wife, Caterina Gattilusi, in August 1442.

The modern bronze statue on the summit commemorates a Lemnian heroine, Maroula, sword in hand: she was a
Byzantine princess—in a long tradition of warlike Lemnian
women—who defended the castle against the Turks in 1476.
The flight of steps which descend steeply from the entrance
of the **church of the Zoödochos Pigi** to the **well** inside the
mound appear to be Venetian in construction.

The hills due south and southeast of Kotsinas form the
area of the now extinct volcano of **Mosychlos**. In earliest
times this was a notably active volcanic area with flam-
ing craters and smoking fumaroles. It was Mosychlos that
gave rise to the island's many epithets (*aithalea*—'smoky'
(Apollonius of Rhodes), *aithaloessa*—' sooty', *amichtha-
loessa*—'wild' and 'inhospitable' (Homer), *pyroessa*—
'fiery', etc.) as well as to the tradition that it was the earth-
ly workshop of the god Hephaestus. The natural, volcanic
heat may also have been instrumental in early human ex-
periments in metallurgy. The area has long featured in the
mythology and economy of the island: it was from here
that the renowned '**Lemnian Earth**' was extracted once a
year.

LEMNIAN EARTH

'*Lemnia sphragis*', also referred to as '*terra miraculosa*' and '*terra sigillata*', was a medicinal soil used in antiquity as an astringent for snakebites and wounds. Its use was revived again in the 16th century, as a treatment for the plague. It is a greasy clay composed of silica, alumina, chalk, magnesia and iron, that was dug with great ceremony once a year in August from a particular depression in the Mosychlos area. In August the springs of the area would almost have been dry and thereby caused the depositing and hardening of mineral clay elements in small pools of baked mud. It was called *terra* '*sigillata*' ('sealed') or *Lemnia* '*sphragis*' (meaning a 'seal impression'), because it was officially stamped and sealed by the priestess of Artemis before being distributed. It has a predominantly red colour (hence the former name for Kotsinas—'*Kokkinos*'—which means 'red'). Galen, who travelled to Lemnos in 167 AD to establish for himself the nature and medicinal usefulness of Lemnian earth, suspected that this colour might have been due to the admixture of goat's blood, but those with whom he spoke told him otherwise. He

was convinced of its effectiveness and says he returned to Rome with several thousand *sphragides*, or
stamped packets, for his own patients. The bole-like
clay contains an active medicinal ingredient, probably an antibacterial and an astringent alum salt of
the kind used in haemostatic, pharmaceutical ap-
plications. Galen (*Opera Omnia*, ed. C.G. Kuhn, xii,
169 et ff.) distinguished three varieties of Lemnian
earth: the medicinal one, prepared by the priestess
herself; a second kind, also red in colour, used as a
pigment (similar to Armenian 'bole'); and a third for
the cleaning of wool and other garments—a kind of
fuller's earth or bentonite.

Fourteen centuries later, Pierre Belon, the 16th
century natural historian from Le Mans in France,
visited Constantinople where he encountered eight-
een different types of clay marketed as 'Lemnian
Earth'. Belon later visited and described how to find
the extraction point on Lemnos. He mentions that
it was 'not more than four arrow-shots away' from
the castle of Kotsinas: 'between the port and the hill
there is a small chapel called St Saviour's, where the
monks gather on the 6th of August, the date set for

the extraction of the earth from its vein. After leaving the church and walking towards the hillock we found two paths, one to the left and one to the right leading to two springs, one about one arrow-shot away from the other'. One of these was probably the spring of Phthelideía, which still exists today. About twenty metres northwest of the spring, are clefts of weathered, pyroclastic rock, which in places has been altered into earths with strong colours: white, yellow and red. The alum and other soluble elements present here may have been washed by rain out of the higher volcanic ground into sedimentary pools in the fields below, which then dried out towards mid-summer.

It is curious in view of the association of the island with the story of Philoctetes and his festering snake-bite, that Lemnos should have become the place where the main remedy for such bites in antiquity was to be found.

To the eastern side of Moschylos is the village of **Repanídi** (5km) grouped around the square in front of the church of **Aghios Giorgios**—a handsome early 20th century building in local stone; directly behind its east end, beside the graveyard, stands its 18th century predecessor—a luminous and airy, apsed hall, with a fine wooden iconostasis. The track down its north side leads to the scattered rural community of **Aghios Ypátios**, immersed in a landscape of unexpected beauty. Bearing left at the chapel of Aghios Nikolaos, dwarfed by the immense oak tree in its enclosure, you come after almost 1.5km to the rural church of **Aghios Athanasios**.

Opposite the path leading to the church is a small **Ottoman fountain**, with primitively carved palm-trees on its face. The church of Aghios Athanasios sits on large ancient blocks which protrude at the front. The small enclosure in front of the church and the exterior walls (south side) include decorative and constructional fragments from an early Byzantine church on the site—capitals, architraves and fragments of *templon* screens. The altar inside is composed of a column base, a statue plinth and a carved slab of a *templon*, laid flat. The site is probably a pagan shrine in origin. Though once an area of volcanic activity there is now little that disturbs the tranquillity except the flocks of doves wheeling in the air. The gently rolling landscape all around and the beautiful, decaying stone farmhouses make this one of the most attractive and tranquil corners of the island.

From Aghios Ypátios a track leads 3.5km due north

towards **Ancient *Hephaistia*,** the other city (with Myrina) of the *di-polis* of Lemnos in ancient times, and the
larger of the two in its heyday. No metalled roads, as yet,
reach Hephaistia which occupies a windswept, treeless
promontory in the bay of Pournia, overlooking an almost
landlocked inlet within the larger bay. Funds from 'en-
hancement programmes' have been lavished on this otherwise remote site, and the use of a towering perimeter
fence and large concreted areas for the theatre has given
it more the appearance of a military installation than an
archaeological treasure. Only a small proportion of the
large area of settlement has so far been explored, and the
points of archaeological interest are widely dispersed over
the hillside. (*Most of the site has unrestricted access, except
for the theatre which is open 8.30–3*)

The site has pre-Greek origins, going back to earliest times.
The local pottery carried Mycenaean/Minoan ceramic traditions into the Geometric period; and finds of imported
wares bear witness to a lively trade with Macedonia, Corinth
and Athens. The first (Italian) archaeological expeditions excavated a necropolis of the 8th and 7th centuries BC (*south of
the neck of the promontory*). They uncovered a sanctuary destroyed by fire during a Persian attack in the last years of the
6th century BC (*west slope of the promontory*), revealing rec-

tangular buildings on two levels and a room endowed with benches along two sides containing broken dedications and parts of the cult statue of a female deity—the 'Great Goddess' of Lemnos—a divinity who was later assimilated with Cybele. To the south of the sanctuary, a residential building unit of the city is currently being excavated (*on the brow directly above the parking lot*) with a level of Hellenistic constructions above Archaic predecessors. Parts of the enceinte of walls can be traced in the northern perimeter, where they circle behind the acropolis (*eastern summit*).

The city reached its greatest extent in Hellenistic times and the conspicuous remains of the large **theatre** (*central west*) date principally from this period. As often happens in settlements which have been repeatedly rebuilt after seismic destructions, archaeologists have found the remains of an Archaic sanctuary and of streets and buildings of the Classical period beneath the Hellenistic *cavea*. It may replace an earlier and much smaller wooden theatre situated on part of the site. The first ten rows of seats in local poros stone belong to the earliest stone theatre-structure, and are of the Late Classical period. This was enlarged in Hellenistic times with more rows of seats and the addition of retaining walls and buttresses. The final modifications—the addition of a more complex *skene* behind the stage—belong to the Roman period.

Beside the shore, near the parking lot, are the remains of a Byzantine **bath-house** complex, now transformed into farm buildings and occupying the site of the earlier, Hellenistic baths. It incorporates several inscribed marble blocks from earlier structures.

In later centuries the city became the seat of a Byzantine bishop, fell to the Venetians in 1204, and around 1395 was partially destroyed by a landslide and subsequently abandoned.

Although unsigned, it is possible to navigate the rough tracks eastwards across country to the deserted hamlet of Aghios Aléxandros where you regain the asphalt road leading to the attractive site of the ***sanctuary of the Cabeiri**, or '*Cabeireion*' (17km from the Varos junction by the main, asphalted road), on the northeastern extremity of the bay of Pourniá (*open daily, 8.30–3.30, except Mon*). The road drops and ends just above the entrance to the sanctuary, at the foot of a flight of steps.

The nature of the sanctuary and its buildings
We are looking here at the site of a cult which is of pre-Greek origin, and at the ruins of buildings which are not temples as such, but a specific and unusual type of structure called a '*telesterion*'—a large, rectangular, covered, assembly-hall

used for the (largely nocturnal) rituals of mystery cults (*see Samothrace, pp. 111–116*). Such a building had few or no windows and was illuminated inside by torches: it was in the form of a hypostyle hall, with benches (sometimes in tiers) against the walls around the edge of a central space where liturgical ceremonies were enacted. The main space is always accompanied by small adjoining rooms. Unlike temples, *telesteria* do not appear to have required a specific, canonical orientation. At this site are the remains of three *telesteria* (two of which on the south terrace are superimposed) dating from the 7th century BC, the 2nd century BC and the 2nd century AD successively.

The Cabeiri

The cult, probably going back to the 8th century BC, predates the Greek presence on the island and was probably brought from Anatolia. It centred on a couple (or group, by some accounts) of divinities called 'the Cabeiri' whose identity is fluid and hard to define with any certainty. Their cult is encountered principally in the Northern Aegean (especially Samothrace, Imbros and Lemnos) and its adjacent mainland, as well as in Boeotia, at Thebes and Anthedon. The Cabeiri are always assistant, rather than principal, divinities (somewhat like *duendes*) but the major divinity with whom they are associated changes: in Boeotian Thebes they were associated with agricultural work and divinities of the land and fertility; in Samothrace they are associated with the Great Mother Goddess; and in Lemnos they appear as smiths, seen later as assistants to—and by some accounts, sons of—Hephaestus. Some scholars suggest their name is related to the Semitic root '*kabir*' ('lord'); others to the Sumerian '*cabar*', meaning copper—which might seem more appropriate given the metallurgic traditions of the island of Lemnos.

Layout of the site

From the foot of the steps you enter the wide, open north terrace, partially cut into the hill at the eastern end and almost completely occupied by the meticulous, isodomic foundations of the 2nd century BC, **Hellenistic *telesterion*—** the second of the three successive structures. The form of the large rectangular hall is clear, with the bases visible of the eight Ionic columns which supported its roof in two rows down the middle. To the western end (nearest the foot of the steps) the hall is bounded by a long corridor and then a series of four small rooms, the larger of which may have been used for ritual banquets. At the opposite end is a long **peristyle** of Doric columns against the slope of the hill finishing at its northern end in an alcove in the natural rock. This—the largest building on the site—may never have been completed and appears to have been violently destroyed in the 2nd century AD perhaps during the struggles between Rome and Philip V of Macedon.

From the southeast corner of the Hellenistic building it is possible to see the massive Archaic supporting wall beneath the terrace on the steep hillside to the south. On this second terrace was both the earliest and the latest *telesterion* on the site, with the remains of the Roman building most visible today built on top of the original Archaic version. In Antiquity access to the area was by a steep and winding path up from the shore, which entered the sanctuary from the south. The design of the **Roman *telesterion*** mimics on a smaller scale that of its Hellenistic predecessor—this time with two rows of five columns (whose bases can be seen) supporting the roof, and with benches on both of the long sides. In similar fashion to the Hellenistic building, there is a lateral space and a series of small rooms at the far (north) end of the hall; these stand in relation to the main space as the sanctuary behind the iconostasis does to the body of an Orthodox church. The Roman structure must have been short lived, since the cult was destroyed in Early Christian times, less than 200 years later.

In 1990 archaeologists brought to light the **Archaic *telesterion*** directly below: this possessed an entrance-portico on the (seaward) west side whose foundations were supported by the massive retaining wall, still visible below. At the south

end of the hall the semicircular projection of stone functioned as a sacred hearth. Crucial for understanding the site
was the discovery of a couple of storage areas at the foot of
the terrace walls which yielded a wealth of sacred libation
vessels, votive figurines and lamps, now mostly in the museum in Myrina.

The choice of the site may be linked to an evocative cave
on the shore below (*access by the stairs beside the guardian's
hut*), known as the **cave of Philoctetes** and linked to the story of the hapless Homeric archer (*see below*).

Visible from the road a little south of the *Cabeireion*, and
even more conspicuous from the sea, on the north side
of Tigani Bay, are the ungainly ruins of the failed *Kaviria
Palace Holiday Complex*.

The peninsula north from the junction at Aghios Aléxandros is an open area of rolling grain fields below long
ridges (occupied mostly by the military), with two busy
communities at its heart—**Panaghía** (18km) and **Plaka**
(20.5km). Water is never far from the surface, causing
breaks of pampas-grass to flourish unexpectedly. A special water or '*aghiasma*' (a 'miraculous spring') rises by
the shore on the coast north and west of Plaka (*2.4km
from Plaka: follow signs for Aghios Charálambos from the
west side of the village and continue 400m along the coast*

beyond the chapel itself. Steps lead down to the spring). The fine, soft-green mud which decants in the two pools to either side of the central (cold) **spring** is used for external application. To the opposite side of the cape, a track leads northeast out of Plaka to the promontory of **Palaiokastro** which is girt with mediaeval fortifications, now in very decayed condition. Due east of here, out to sea, is the sunken Charos Reef—which may possibly have been the islet of *Chryse* in Antiquity.

PHILOCTETES & THE ISLET OF 'CHRYSE'

Amongst the Greeks who sailed to Troy was the famed archer Philoctetes who, according to Sophocles, possessed the bow and arrows of Hercules. Apparently, while sacrificing to Apollo or to another divinity, he was bitten by a venomous snake and was left behind by his comrades because of the putrefying stench of the subsequently infected and gangrenous wound. Homer (*Iliad*, II. 722) says that Philoctetes was left on Lemnos; according to Proclus, the Greeks were feasting on the island of Tenedos at the time the incident occurred; and Sophocles in his *Philoctetes* explains how the accident happened neither on Lemnos nor Tenedos, but on an island called 'Chryse' where a goddess of that name was worshipped. He says that the serpent which bit Philoctetes was the guardian of her shrine (*Phil.* 263–270 & 1326–1328). Pausanias, corroborating Sophocles's version, goes on to add more uncertainty to the story in a passage in which he is commenting on the power of destiny to destroy great sanctuaries and cities in the course of history while sparing others (*Descrip.* VIII.33.4). 'No long sail from Lemnos', he writes, 'was once an island—Chryse—where, it is said, Philoctetes met with his accident from the water-snake. But the waves utterly overwhelmed it and Chryse sank and disappeared in the depths ... So temporary and utterly weak are the fortunes of men.' Pausanias does not say when this happened; but the historian, Appian, mentions a 'deserted island near Lemnos ... where an altar of Philoctetes, a bronze serpent, a bow and a breastplate bound with fillets—the memorials of his sufferings' were still to be seen as late as the 1st century BC.

Was this 'deserted island' in fact Aghios Efstratios? Or has 'Chryse' really disappeared beneath the sea? Intrigued by a large, possibly sunken land mass known as the Charos Reef which is marked on Admiralty charts lying to the east of Lemnos, an Italian submarine explorer, Piero Nicola Gargallo, began in 1960 to examine the floor of the bank which he found to be strewn with fragments of pottery. At a depth of about 13m, he claims to have found rectangular white stone blocks, which could represent the remains of the sanctuary on Chryse, and might substantiate what Pausanias suggested of its fate. The reef is located about 10 nautical miles east of Cape Petsiá in northeast Lemnos; its coordinates are 39.91'7"°N/25.55'0"°E.

One of the low summits of this northeastern promontory of Lemnos must be the mount '*Hermaeon*' referred to by Aeschylus (*Agamemnon*, 281 ff.) where one of the first fire-beacons was lit in the chain which Clytemnestra had ordered so that a signal announcing the fall of Troy could be transmitted to her in Mycenae. The chain began on Mount Ida above Troy, passed to Lemnos, then on to the peak of Athos, and so down, via several links, to Cithaeron and thence into the Peloponnese.

The road south from Plaka and Panaghia to Kontopoúli, passes a large salt-water lagoon—**Límni Alykí**—the largest of three which occupy the central eastern coast of the island. These are important, wetland **wildlife-pre-serves** with high populations of migrating birds in season—a variety of waders, Wood- and Green-sandpipers, and terns. Winter visitors include flocks of Shelduck and Greater flamingo, and among the resident birds are Avocets, Stone-curlew, Black-winged stilts and Fan-tailed warblers, with the rarer Ruddy shelduck (distinguishable by its all-over, red-brown body and pale-tan head with dark collar) breeding here in small numbers. Though rarely exceeding 200m in altitude, the rolling plains of the east of Lemnos are never dull in any season—always teeming with partridge, guinea-fowl and singing larks; in spring they are a mass of wild flowers; and even in the driest months they are full of aromatic and colourful wild chrysanthemum.

The area between Kontopoúli and Repanídi is given special character by its sparse and monumental oak-trees. The villages themselves are also of interest and character: **Kontopoúli** (8km) is well-known for its pottery and **Kaliópi** (9.5km) for its saddle-less horse-riders who race in honour of the feast of St George in late April; at **Romanoú** (6.5km) there are half a dozen ruined windmills of the 18th century on the hill above the village. The symmetrical, often cuboid, stone houses and churches with broad façades are also characteristic of the area.

SOUTH BRANCH

The principal administrative centre of the southeast of
Lemnos is the town of **Moúdros** (*8km from Varos junction
by the south branch*), due east of which (500m) lies the
island's largest **war cemetery**. In the centre of the walled
area is the French cenotaph; to the east, that of the Com-
monwealth countries; in the corners, the Muslim labourers and the fallen of the Indian army are commemorated;
and in the southeast extremity is one lone, earlier grave
to a mute, inglorious Brooke—the 22 year-old stoker of
HMS *Trafalgar* who died in 1893. The armistice between
Turkey and the Allied Forces of October 1918 was signed
on board HMS *Agamemnon* anchored to the west of here
in Moudros Bay.

Off the east shore of the bay, 1km north of Moudros,
is **Koukonisi** attached by a causeway across the shallow waters. The low islet—much frequented today by
curlews—has the remains of a **prehistoric settlement**
(*currently covered*) of the Early and Middle Bronze Age,
where important finds have been made pointing to Lemnos's significance in the context of Mycenaean trade and
expansion. It is situated at the highest point towards the
northern end of the islet.

Across the ridge of hills from Moudros on the east

coast of the island, at **Polióchni* (15.5km), lies one of Europe's most important prehistoric sites, and perhaps the continent's earliest organised urban settlement. Although pre-dating the Great Pyramid and Stonehenge by many centuries, and much larger and more complex in organisation than the remarkable hamlet of Skara Brae in Orkney, Polióchni came onto the scene more than three millennia after Çatal Hüyük in Anatolia had established itself as what many consider to be the world's first known urban complex.

The settlement covers a large area on top of a low cliff at the end of a long curving bay which is tucked under a promontory offering shelter from the north winds. The natural characteristics of the site—beautiful, but not dramatic—are strangely reminiscent in configuration of prehistoric Phylakopí on Milos. Excavations in 1931–36 by Alessandro della Seta of the Italian School of Archaeology uncovered four principal, successive settlements: an unfortified town of the Late Bronze Age, beneath which lay a city of the Copper Age, with two earlier Neolithic cities further below. The earliest (4th millennium BC) is believed to pre-date Troy. While undoubtedly of primary interest to the specialist, the site impresses the amateur visitor nonetheless with its extent and organisation, and comprises a number of striking monuments and constructions.

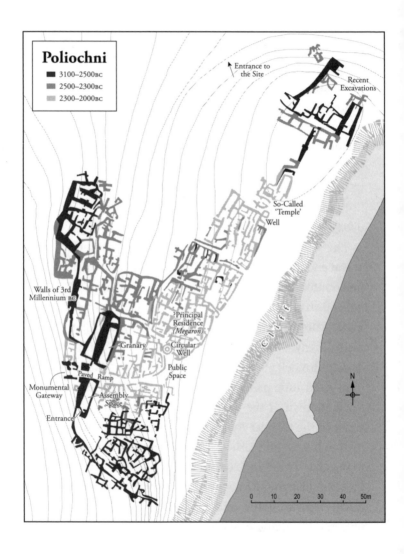

Poliochni

- 3100–2500BC
- 2500–2300BC
- 2300–2000BC

Entrance to
the Site

Recent
Excavations

So-Called
'Temple'

Well

Walls of 3rd
Millennium BC

?Principal
Residence
(Megaron)

Granary

Circular
Well

Public
Space

Paved Ramp

Monumental
Gateway

Assembly
Space

Entrance

CLIFF

N

0   10   20   30   40   50m

HISTORY

First inhabited around 4,500 BC by settlers coming from the coast of Asia Minor opposite, the site initially consisted of a village of huts of roughly elliptical form. Throughout the 4th millennium BC it steadily grew, acquiring terracing, retaining- and fortification- walls, streets, assembly spaces and public buildings, which bear witness to a high level of social organisation and urban development. Dwellings began to be organised into blocks and to acquire a more structured, *megaron*-type form, with a square plan and an antechamber. The site possessed good water (two plentiful wells) and was situated at the mouth of the Avlaki torrent which irrigated and rendered fertile a broad valley inland of the town. To the north, Cape Droskopos provided shelter for a rudimentary harbour. In the widest context, the site was ideally placed to be a bridge between the civilised world of the Near Eastern mainland and a Europe as yet still ignorant of urban organisation. Around 2,100 BC the settlement was abandoned after a catastrophic earthquake. During the following millennium—while its neighbour, Troy, flourished preeminently—Polióchni remained a drastically reduced settlement clustered around the wells of fresh water on the hill-top.

Visit to the site

An itinerary is suggested here which is contrary to the general direction indicated on the site, but has the virtue of being more chronologically coherent and starting with the earliest and most impressive monumental remains. By heading for the furthest point below and to the right-hand (west) side of the excavated area as viewed from the site-entrance, you will come to the **earliest monumental gate** to the city (4th millennium BC), after passing beside the long brow of the later, mid-3rd millennium BC **walls**. The early gate is clearly recognisable from the impressively **paved ramp** (3rd millennium BC) that leads up through it into the city between two gate-bastions. To the left-hand side as you enter and climb up, is a deep, rectangular **grain-store**: this would have been a covered and closed structure, amply protected by the ramparts into which it is built.

Opposite it to the right (south) is the *assembly space, the earliest example of such a communal facility yet found in Europe. Roughly rectangular in shape, with stone seats accommodating approximately 50 people along one side, and a separate, apse-like adjunct at the south end through which the building was entered, this may have been the meeting place for the fifty or so elders of the family nuclei of the community. At the summit to the left is one of the settlement's two principal **wells**—circular in form and lined with stones to a considerable depth, constituting a notable example of early engineering. An open paved area surrounds the well which functioned as the early town's main **square**; to the north side is one of the largest of the *megaron* buildings which, because of its prominent size and position, has often been considered to be a ruler's residence. This hypothesis has been given support by the finding in an adjacent room (*no. 643*) of the only hoard of gold jewellery which has so far been unearthed in Polióchni. Some of the pieces are on display in the museum in Myrina; the remainder are in Athens. The side rooms of the large *megaron* also contain sunken storage vases. The building and the surrounding area date from the last epoch before the earthquake of c. 2000 BC.

The main street of the settlement continues north along the eastern edge of the hill to a second square, this time with a well of square section, similarly lined with stone blocks. Across an open space and to the north stood a rectangular building conspicuous by its size and relative isolation. This has often been called a '**temple**', but no specifically cultic finds have been made on its site. The fine and distinct layer of large monoliths laid flat at its base beneath the walls distinguish it from other buildings on the site. At the northern extremity of the excavations are the bases of walls and buildings uncovered in the last two decades: amongst those that have come to light is a large building with a central pilaster and a stone bench around the inside wall, which may also be seen as the seat of the community's most powerful person.

To the south of Polióchni and Kamínia (the village where the Lemnos Stele was found—*see below*) the landscape is as tranquil, open and treeless as that of a Hebridean island. There are grain fields, grazing flocks, skylarks, breaks of pampas, and long deserted and unprotected bays—culminating in the finest between Aghios Sozon and the southern tip of the island. The two villages of **Phisíni** (20km) and **Skandáli** (21.5km) are a pleasing mix of old and new buildings, dilapidated ruins and well-kempt, flowering terraces. From the east side of the principal road, 500m north of Phisíni, a track bears off and proceeds due north, for over a kilometre to the **Phisíni Towers**, a curious and unexpected site commanding excellent views of the east coast and of the sea to the south. The two towers—now mounds of collapsed stone—crown the ridge, perfectly aligned on a north/south axis, with a walled enclosure still perceivable to the west. Both towers are square in plan (c. 10m x 10m), but their masonry is noticeably different. The north tower has rectangular cut masonry which could even be late Hellenistic (although not fully consonant with the standard masonry of the period), while the south tower has more clearly mediaeval masonry. Large monoliths are incorporated in the perimeter wall. The north tower may be an ancient watch-tower which was later incorporated into the small mediaeval, fortified settlement: the terracing and fallen masonry on the hillside below suggests a substantial community. On the hill to the west are other ruined buildings and windmills.

THE LEMNOS *STELE*

Herodotus's comments (*Hist.* I. 94) on the origins of the Etruscans have given rise to continuous academic debate. The Lydians, he states, claimed that after a period of protracted famine their king sent half of their population away to emigrate from their homeland in Asia Minor and to seek a new life elsewhere under the guidance of his son Tyrrhenus, and that they settled in Umbria in Italy calling themselves 'Tyrrhenians', and being subsequently known as Etruscans. Dionysius of Halicarnassus (*Ant. Rom.* I 25–30), by contrast, in a thoughtful and lucidly argued critique of the sources available to him, later concluded that their origins were autochthonous. Since then the debate has never died, although the prevailing thinking today is to favour the latter over the former, since it

better accords with the archaeological facts. Dionysius goes on, however, to underline how curiously
unrelated the Etruscan language is to any other in
what we now call the Indo-European group: in fact
our knowledge of it is still only partial.

It was of particular significance therefore when,
in 1885, the demolition of a church near Kamínia
brought to light a stone *stele* inscribed with a lettering remarkably similar to the Etruscan inscriptions
found in Italy. The *stele* in fact bears a late 6th century BC inscription (*IG*, 12.8.1) in the native Lemnian language. It has now been deciphered (it is the
epitaph of a man who lived and worked in the ter-
ritory of Myrina) and bears very close affinities to
the Etruscan language. There is an undeniable link,
therefore, between Lemnos and Etruria—added to
which they also share specific burial customs and
a preeminence in matters metallurgical. Etruscans
were good mariners and it is not impossible that, as
some have argued, Lemnos was a kind of commercial colony of theirs—in other words that there was
a migration in the opposite direction to that implied
by Herodotus. But so early? Interesting and very re-

cent DNA research has suggested that a number of the mitochondrial DNA lineages of both natives of communities of Etruscan origin in Italy, and Tuscan cattle breeds, occur nowhere else in Europe and are shared only with those found in the Near East.

PRACTICAL INFORMATION

814 00 Lemnos: area 476 sq.km; perimeter 263km; resident population 17,545; max. altitude 430m. Port Authority: T. 22540 22225. **Travel and information**: Lemnos Municpality, www.lemnos-island.com; Petrides Travel, T. 22540 22208.

ACCESS

By air: Lemnos is generally served by two daily flights with *Olympic Air* throughout the year from Athens, and five weekly flights to Thessaloniki. The airport is in the middle of the island at a distance of 18.5km from Myrina (€15 by taxi).

By boat: Ferry connections are less convenient since so many of the boats arrive and leave in the middle of the night. Both **SAOS Ferries** and **NEL Lines** between them link Myrina with the North Aegean port of Kavala 6 times weekly, and with Lavrion (for Athens) 3 times a week (via Aghios Efstratios); their other route links Lemnos to Mytilene 3 times a week, and to Chios and Samos once weekly. **GA Ferries** run 4 weekly connections to Mytilene and Chios; 2 to Thessaloniki, and 1 a week to Alexandroupolis and Kavala to the north, and to Rhodes and the Dodecanese to the south. The *F/B Aeolis* plies the route between Myrina and Aghios Efstratios daily except Saturday and Sunday, leaving Aghios Efstratios at 6.30 each morning, and returning from Myrina at 3 pm.

LODGING

The most characterful place to stay in Myrina is the **Archontiko Hotel** *(T. 22540 29800-1, fax 23330)* one block in from the north beach, between the shore and Od. Kyda, the main street of the old town. The hotel is in a traditional Thracian-style mansion of 1814, as its name implies, with pleasantly furnished rooms. The **Nefeli Apartments** *(T. 22540 23351, fax 24041)*, which occupy the highest building on the slope of the castle, are a more modern and panoramic alternative; the apartments are run as an adjunct to the café below which has splendid views over the town. The rooms are spacious and comfortable, and a good breakfast is served in the café. There are many small pensions in the town, too: one of the nicest is the **Romeikos Yialos** *(T. 22540 23787, fax 22197)* in Sachtouri street behind the north beach.

EATING

In Myrina, **Glaros**, overlooking the south harbour with a pleasing view has good home-cooking of fresh fish and vegetables, and serves a local retsina produced on the island. Just in from the north shore on Aiolou St, the *mezedopoleion* '**Siniálo**' is particularly good for its variety of salads, *mezés* and vegetable dishes, and probably represents the best quality in the town.

Wine on Lemnos is produced mostly in the area around Aghios Dimitrios, with a grape variety that imparts an unusually flowery quality to its nose, which compensates for a shortness of flavour. It can be found in the older tavernas right across the island, especially in the smaller villages. The small, friendly tavernas in both the *plateias* of Kamínia, near Poliochni, and of Platy, just south of Myrina, are good places to sample it.

FURTHER READING

'*L'enigma svelato della lingua etrusca*' by Giulio Facchetti (Rome, 2000) is an erudite and fascinating commentary (awaiting translation into English) on the Lemnos *Stele* and its contribution to understanding the language of the Etruscans.

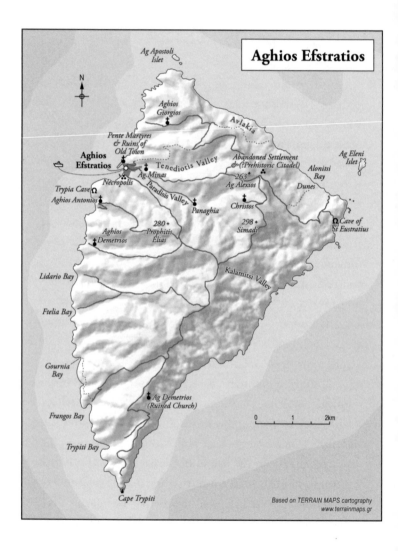

Aghios Efstratios

Ag Apostoli Islet

N

Aghios Giorgios

Avlakia

Pente Martyres & Ruins of Old Town

Aghios Efstratios

Tenediotis Valley

Abandoned Settlement (?Prehistoric Citadel)

Ag Eleni Islet

Alonitsi Bay

Ag Minas

Necropolis

263 Ag Alexios

Dunes

Trypia Cave

Paradisis Valley

Aghios Antonios

Panaghia

Christos

Cave of St Eustratius

Aghios Demetrios

280 Prophitis Élias

298 Simadi

Lidario Bay

Kalamitsi Valley

Ftelia Bay

Gournia Bay

Ag Demetrios (Ruined Church)

Frangos Bay

0   1   2km

Trypiti Bay

Cape Trypiti

Based on TERRAIN MAPS cartography
www.terrainmaps.gr

AGHIOS EFSTRATIOS

Aghios Efstratios remains perhaps the least known and least visited of the medium-sized islands of the Aegean. Riding adrift in wide open waters at the centre of the sea, equidistant from the Greek and Asian mainlands and almost midway between Mount Athos and Lesbos, its lack of close neighbours and the absence of that all-important proximity to a reassuring land-mass has combined to leave the island solitary and unincluded. In the Aegean world proximity counts for everything—the critical closeness of one island to others in a similar group as in the Cyclades, or to the centres of a mainland coast as in the case of the islands of the Dodecanese and Sporades, is what drives the cultural and commercial traffic that brings prosperity and evolution. Throughout much of its history that traffic, that life-giving activity and exchange, just passed Aghios Efstratios by. It circulated around it instead, and many of those who ended up on the island did so only accidentally because they had been blown off-course. There was a small city on the island in Classical antiquity, whose name is not known to us; but for long periods after that era, the island was either abandoned or used as a training ground for novice monks destined ultimately to return and settle on Mount Athos. On clear days Athos is just visible from Aghios Efstratios; so also are Lemnos and, sometimes, Skyros; but often the island looks out onto a clear and unbroken horizon of water on all sides—which is a rare and somewhat disquieting sensation in the habitually close-knit world of the Aegean Islands.

Although constantly a prey to emigration, a small community of farmers and fishermen extracted a living on the island throughout the 18th and 19th centuries and into the early part of the 20th century, creating a small town which was a pleasing cascade of balconied, Thracian-style houses on the hill above the port. Then, on 20 February 1968, disaster struck. The small settlement was razed to the ground by an earthquake whose epicentre was under the sea to the north of the island. The earthquake, of magnitude 7.1 on the Richter scale, struck in the early hours of the morning, destroying the majority of the stone and timber-frame houses and killing many in their sleep. Earthquakes are a common phenomenon in the Aegean area, and the inured Greek islanders are generally not slow to re-group and re-build their communities after such disasters. The particular misfortune for Aghios Efstratios was timing; the quake occurred during the years of the military regime of the Colonels, who had for some time taken advantage of the island's remoteness by using it as a penal colony for the exile and hospitalisation of political undesirables—among them, for a brief period, the poet Yannis Ritsos. There was little incentive for the authorities therefore to give intelligent support to the struggling islanders. Contrary to the wishes of many who would have salvaged their houses and reconstructed them, orders were given that what remained standing should be bulldozed and, with the delivery of materials for over 130 pre-fabricated, cement box-dwellings, the remaining inhabitants were moved 'for their own safety' from the hillside where their families had lived for decades, and relocated in the humid hollow inland of the harbour, where their gardens had been thitherto. Photographic images taken in the summer of 1968 of the serried ranks of military shelters, say everything about the awfulness of that decision.

In the last couple of decades, new vegetation, human wear and tear, and the innate ability of the Greeks to embellish even the most unprepossessing spot with a flowering *avlí*, has modified and softened the visual impact of the pre-fabricated colony. Today a cluster of restored pre-earthquake houses by the port and some bright Aegean colours greet the arriving visitor at the harbour, and the abrasive military lay-out has somehow softened.

The poignant story of the earthquake and its aftermath is touched on in a thoughtful and fascinating new museum which has been created in the town principally to record the life of the political exiles here—who often greatly outnumbered the locals.

Visitors not afraid to walk a lot and to be content with the simplest lodgings and food, will find in this island a bounty of fine landscapes, completely untrammeled by modernity. Aghios Efstratios has scarcely any springs and its terrain is rough, rocky and volcanic: but miraculously and unexpectedly, many of the slopes are well-wooded with oaks, and some of its beautifully folded ravines and inlets are of great intimacy. There is a tranquillity in them that can only be dreamed of on other islands.

HISTORY

The modern name of the island, which is abbreviated locally to '*Aï Stratis*' comes from St Eustratius, a holy figure from Bythinia who took hermitic refuge from the persecutions of the Iconoclastic period in a cave on the island early in the 9th century. But the island's name in antiquity is uncertain: some ascribe the Homeric name '*Chryse*'('gold[en]') to the island (*see above pp. 50–52*); others identify it as Ancient *Halonnesos*. Much later, the island is mentioned by the 16th century Turkish admiral, Piri Reis, under the appellation 'Boz[1] Papas'—the first word a reference to its lack of cultivation, the second to its monastic ownership.

Evidence of a possible Mycenaean presence has been pointed to on the central east coast of the island, in the area of Aghios Alexios; but the main centre of habitation in historic times was just east of the present port on the hill of Aghios Minas. Surface finds from Hellenistic and Byzantine times have come to light at other points on the island. In 1021 Basil II, the 'Bulgar-slayer', granted the island to the monastery of the Great Lavra on Mount Athos,

[1]'*Boz*' and '*bozca*'—primarily meaning 'grey'—are both used in Turkish to refer to uncultivated land.

to be a training ground for its young monks. Their presence was always a prey to pirate attack, and Cristoforo Buondelmonti who stopped on the island in 1418 refers to the island as a place of pirates. In the late 16th and early 17th centuries, the settlement on the hillside north of the harbour was established. The limitations of water and fertility meant that the population was never large: in the mid-20th century it must have numbered a maximum of about 800 residents. But the island's use as a penal colony for political prisoners from 1928 right through to 1968, at times pushed the temporary population well over 3,000. Evidence of some of the improvised camps can still be seen. In 1968 the earthquake destroyed the town: both before and after this catastrophe, many of the islanders emigrated to Australia.

In 2009 an ambitious (and perhaps ultimately fantastic) project was mooted to turn Aghios Efstratios into Europe's first entirely 'green' island, with its residents relying on nothing but renewable sources of energy for all domestic and transportation needs.

THE HARBOUR & TOWN

Perhaps the single most determining factor for the island's isolation has been its lack of any good, all-weather harbour. Ferry-boats have only been able to dock on the island since 1997 when the harbour mole was completed. Before that time all goods and passengers had to be transferred by small skiffs that ran between the shore and the ferry which would momentarily ride water at a safe distance from the port. This meant that, in the frequent periods of rough weather and wind, the island was inaccessible.

The town of **Aghios Efstratios** lies at the mouth of the principal western valley, which is formed by the confluence of two streams—the Tenediótis to the north, and the Paradísis to the south. The small hill directly to the east of the town which rises between the two watercourses was the site of the **ancient settlement**. Today the hill is crowned by the (rebuilt) chapel of **Aghios Minas**, which contains in its enclosure a simple monument to the political exiles who died on the island during their internment, the majority of whom perished in the particularly hard winter of 1941/42. Of the ancient town itself, there is little of antiquity to see above the surface beyond some

vestigial stretches of ancient retaining-wall built in Les-
bian-style masonry on the western slope. But there are
sherds of Classical, Hellenistic and Roman pottery visible
on the surface all around. Even a cursory search will re-
veal these—many of them pieces of black-glaze pottery,
probably of Attic origin.

Since the late 16th century the main settlement has
been situated on the south slope of the hill to the north
of the harbour. The small cemetery church on its summit may be built on the side of a mediaeval lookout post.
To its west along the ridge, are the remnants of a line of
windmills, destroyed in the earthquake; some of the mill-
wheels can still be seen on site, constructed from pieces of
re-used—and possibly antique—masonry bound by iron
rings into improvised wheels. At the western point of the
ridge, directly above the harbour is the collapsed church
of the **Pente Martyres**, which was a late-17th century
foundation in origin. The debris of its collapsed roof has
recently been cleared, revealing the original plan of the
building which had a quadrant of monolithic columns
of Proconnesian marble supporting the roof. Two of
them are still visible—one bearing an eroded Byzantine
inscription—plus a third, made from plastered cement,
in imitation. One of the door-posts of ancient marble is
still in place, and a single marble block before the thresh-

old still bears the incised design of its circular decoration with some pieces of the inlaid mosaic embellishment still visible.

From the church a stone path winds down through the midst of the ruins of stone-built, Thracian-style houses; some of them still contain their fine interior woodwork which, in places, is left open to the skies. A few of the older buildings have been rehabilitated beside the harbour, with their characteristic, protruding, timber-frame upper floors. Other survivors of the earthquake of 1968, stand along the lower slope of the hill to the east. Almost at the foot of the hill and a little way inland from the harbour is the church of **Aghios Vasilios**—the only church to survive the earthquake in reasonable shape. An original marble plaque immured into the upper west façade of the building gives the church's date of founding as 1727: the date is expressed, with inimitable Byzantine complexity by the letters '*ΑΨΚΖ*' in the bottom right hand corner. The building is a (curiously) apse-less, rectangular hall surmounted by a low cupola on a central drum.

Further inland along the hillside can be seen the long symmetrical façade of the **Maraslios-Logothetios School-building** of 1908 which dominates the eastern end of the village from above. The building has been consolidated and the large, balconied portico on its back side reconstructed. The new school now lies below on the floor of the valley; between the two, a small building—which once housed the earliest school of all and then functioned as an infirmary for the political exiles of the 1940s and '50s—has been restored and turned into a small museum; just below it, a granite column and other antique fragments have been exposed in an undisturbed plot.

The newly opened **Museum of Democracy** (*open daily, except Mon, 10.30–1 & 2–5, www.mouseiodimokratias.gr*) tells the story of the internal political and social upheavals that beset Greece in the period before and after the Second World War, seen from the point of view of the many workers, artesans and intellectuals, both men and women, who were exiled not just on Aghios Efstratios but also on the other smaller islands that were used for reclusion, such as Anafi, Sikinos, Folegandros, Kimolos, Amorgos, Gyaros, Makronisos, and so forth. The small exhibition is absorbing and moving.

The majority of the material is photographic and of the highest quality. The images speak for themselves; but the clear and thoughtful displays give a measured and unstrident commentary on them, leaving the visitor free to form personal conclusions about this tormented period of Greek history. What shines through is how, even in the greatest adversity and privation, the creative spirit could still prevail in a grim internment camp such as this: an improvised theatre created by the detainees with ingenious stage-sets, the production of simple clothing and furniture, and even the extraordinary fashioning of a violin and other instruments from the few materials available so as to create some possibility of music and dance. Both the appalling image of political repression and the hopeful image of the resilience of the human spirit remain vividly with the visitor from the exhibition.

The museum's leaflet suggests an itinerary for visiting the area of the **former internment camp**. This involves following the left-hand branch of the road at the east end of the town (up the Tenediótis water-course), past the exiles' bakery, kitchens and workshops, towards the area where the indoor and outdoor theatres were improvised and the tent-villages were laid out.

Both the watercourses leading east from the village to either side of Aghios Minas hill are surprisingly fertile, with some fruit cultivation and a low cover of poplar trees. The two small churches dedicated to the Panaghia in the valley of the Paradísis to the south, have pleasing settings but are not of historical note.

Returning back towards the shore—in the *plateia* of

the village, a grey limestone memorial, modelled on the form of the 'Victory of Samothrace', commemorates the islanders who died in the two World Wars. Further down by the harbour, is a captured Venetian cannon bearing the date, 1764. On the south side of the bay are vestiges of an ancient (probably Hellenistic) **necropolis**. The hillside is made of a friable, shingle-stone conglomerate and contains some natural holes; but there are a number of larger tombs cut into the rock with neatly finished interiors, especially on the lower east side.

In the headland to the south of the bay are two caves—Gaidarospilia and **Trypia**. The latter, which is only accessible by boat, has two entrances which are the scene of a traditional ritual visit by locals in caïques on Easter Sunday every year.

AROUND THE ISLAND

The island consists of an undulating plateau of hills of roughly uniform height, which folds into seasonally watered valleys on the western side with sparsely scattered oak trees, and drops more dramatically to the sea on the eastern side where the tree cover is much more dense. The oak trees themselves are of particular beauty: they are the **Valonia** or '**Royal**' **Oaks**—*Quercus ithaburensis* (or *Aegylops*) *macrolepis*—which grow in such profusion and to such magnitude on Kea (*see vol 19, pp. 52–54*). Here they are of smaller proportions because of the lesser availability of surface water. The fact that they grow so thickly on the northeast slopes of the island suggests that for much of the year their sustenance comes simply from the moisture in the night- and morning- air, from which such slopes benefit. The trees produce large acorns set in ample, bushy 'collars'. These were the island's principal export in the past, both for animal fodder and for the leather factories of Lesbos, where a dark, tannin-rich liquid extracted from the acorn was used in the preparation of skins. The oaks were economically important to the islanders and the possession of a certain number of trees was frequently an element stipulated in testamentary documents and marriage contracts. Apart from the oaks, vegetation on the island is sparse, with only the valleys that descend to the shore illuminated with swathes of flowering oleander in season.

The terrain of the island is rough and volcanic and is close geologically to the western extremity of Lesbos— the area inland of Sigri. It is best explored by following the existing vehicle tracks. Since the island has virtually no traffic the walker has no disturbance.

Exploring the north of the island

Take the track which begins along the right-hand side of the emergency services' helipad to the north of the port. After 20 minutes the isolated, white chapel of Aghios Giorgios is visible across the valley to the north: this is a very simple, 19th century, stone chapel with a finely-raftered roof and plain interior. It is reached by taking two subsequent left branches in the track—the whole walk taking under an hour from the town. At the second of these junctions (after 40 minutes), you are on the panoramic watershed of the island: by continuing straight at this junction you descend to a small goat pen and then down into the thickest oak groves on the island. The shaded path leads on down to the area of **Avlákia** (a further 30 minutes) on a plateau above the north coast which was considerably cultivated for crops in earlier centuries.

Exploring the east of the island

Follow the track that leads uphill from the town around the southern side of the hill of Aghios Minas. This is a barren and shadeless climb to the watershed which is reached (by continuing always east) after 50 minutes. From this point a magnificent view of the wide bay of Alonitsi, backed by sand dunes opens before you. Behind, and to the west, is the hill of Aghios Alexios; to the south is the summit of **Mount Simadi** (298m), with below it on a spur of the hill (visible to the south-west) the church of **Christós**. This is another (possibly late-18th century) stone church of great simplicity with a rustic and pleasingly carved screen inside. The church was re-roofed after the earthquake, but conserves in its façade a couple of inscribed plaques from the original building, as well as one new one.

Looking northwards from the junction at the watershed, you see a steep and curiously eroded outcrop of rock, with the remains of man-made walls running along the ridge to its right (southeast). The site is interesting and reveals on close examination a large paved area supported by retaining walls below (to the south) and the remains of collapsed stone-buildings—one particularly large structure being probably a former church. Without proper archaeological examination, a date is difficult to ascribe to these remains; but they do not appear to be from a period earlier than the 17th century and are probably what is left of a small farming community. But the site is so strategic and panoramic that it is hard not to suppose a previous, much earlier presence here—perhaps an early **prehistoric citadel** on this natural 'acropolis'. Some of the cuts in the rock outcrop could well date from such an epoch. The only evidence for a Mycenaean presence on the island relates to the hill of Aghios Alexios which rises to its summit (now occupied by the military) a mere 200m to the west.

From the watershed the track leads down into the wide bowl of ***Alonítsi Bay**. Beyond the long sandy shore (reached in a further 35 minutes from the watershed) is the islet of Aghia Eleni, just out to sea to the east. The upper slopes of this amphitheatre of hills are wooded with oak; but the lower areas were once covered with the island's vineyards, which profited from the well-drained and mineral-rich volcanic soil. All that remain today are the eroded signs of terracing. At the far end of the bay is a hill forming the eastern extremity of the island; on its southern side is a limestone outcrop with a modern chapel built in its lee. From the chapel it is possible to fol-

low the path round to the south to the **cave of St Eustratius**, after whom the island is named—sometimes called
'Eustratius the Wonder worker' to distinguish him from
St Eustratius 'the Great', who was a 4th century martyr.
St Eustratius came to the island from his native Bythinia
perhaps as early as 813 in order to escape the persecutions
of Iconclasm. The cave here was his hermitage and refuge until he left the island, possibly for Mount Athos. The
saint rightly chose a place with a deeply inspiring view.
The return from here to the town takes a little over two
hours.

Exploring the south of the island

Take the road which heads uphill to the southeast from
the southern corner of the town, close to the necropolis.
By continuing on east past two turns to the right which
lead back down to the west coast at the bays of Aghios
Antonios and Aghios Demetrios, you reach the watershed
beside a small wind-pump after 35 minutes. Below the
next junction, the steep ravine of **Kalamítsi**, once home
to a small farming village, drops to the east coast below.
As the main track continues south along the ridge of the
island—sometimes to the west and sometimes to the east
of the watershed—the views over the landscape unfold
widely and beautifully, with the single masses of the oak-

trees standing out against the pale volcanic earth, and the faint outline of the Sporades sometimes visible on the southwestern horizon.

At several points the bays down on the west coast can be glimpsed—the wide strand of **Lidarió** (50 minutes from the second junction after the summit of the track, or c. 2 hours 10 minutes total from the town), or the intimate cove of **Frángos Bay** (25 minutes from the third junction and a total of 2 hours 25 minutes from the town). Fifteen minutes beyond the third junction, a painted sign indicates the chapel of **Aghios Demetrios** up to the left. The tiny, collapsed church is on the summit above, with only a small shrine standing in its open sanctuary today: next to it, on the saddle just below, are the ruined walls and foundations of a small, extinct farming community which overlooked the southern promontory of the island. From this point on, the oak trees do not grow any more; the hillsides are as bare as the sea all around—yet their surfaces are still creased with the eroded terracing of past centuries of cultivation.

PRACTICAL INFORMATION

815 00 Aghios Efstratios: area 47.3 sq.km; perimeter 17km; resident population 305; max. altitude 298 m. **Port Authority**: T. 22540 93393.

ACCESS

Of the main-line services, only **NEL Lines** offer 2 weekly connections with the island on their Kavala, Lemnos, Lavrion (Athens) route, with a stop in the middle of the night on Aghios Efstratios. The most practical access is the service which runs between the island and Lemnos (2hrs) on the *F/B Aeolis* which runs daily, except Sat and Sun, leaving Myrina at 3 pm, and returning from Aghios Efstratios at 6.30 each morning. For information: T. 22540 22460 (Myrina) and T. 22540 93414 (Aghios Efstratios)

LODGING

Xenonas Aï Strati (*T. 22540 93393*) overlooking the village, and **Malama Rooms** (*T 22540 93209*) in the lower area near the harbour, both offer simple but adequately furnished rooms.

EATING

The choice of places to eat has now reduced over the last few years from three to one;

Veranda, the café above the harbour is the only fully-fledged taverna left. *Mezes* accompanying drinks are served in the *ouzeri* opposite.

FURTHER READING

'*Ai Stratis—Photographic Images: 1940–70*' from the Vasilios Manikakis archive, published by the Ministry of the Aegean (Mytilene, 2000), is a fascinating photographic reportage of the island in the middle of the last century. The photographs are fine and the portrait of the island outlined by them is haunting.

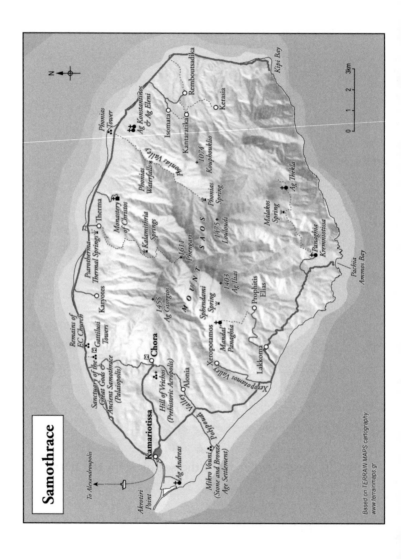

Samothrace

Based on TERRAIN MAPS cartography
www.terrainmaps.gr

SAMOTHRACE

More than any other small island, Samothrace has a solitude and grandeur that are epic. Its rugged gorges and peaks, its trees, waters, winds and shores, are not overwhelming or unwelcoming, but they possess something of the primeval simplicity and the scale of epic. Its forests are those evoked by Homer; its winds are those that propelled and tormented Odysseus; the view from the summit of Mount Saos is the view that Poseidon had of the battle of Troy. Few islands leave so deep and clear and sober an image in the mind as Samothrace. It is perhaps no surprise therefore that an important and very ancient cult of un-nameable and mysterious 'Great Gods' should have evolved here on the slopes of Mount Saos. It was for this that the island was famous in Antiquity. The excavated remains of the Sanctuary of the Great Gods are unusual and little visited. Few Greek sites raise so many important questions which yet remain unanswered.

The massif of Mount Saos is an area of great fascination; its image, either from the sea or from the narrow rim of the island's habitation, is rarely static—often foreboding, occasionally serene, always majestic. At night it enters a new level of existence: not by accident is its

summit called Phengári, 'the moon'. The island consists
of little but the mountain; the sea has conceded a ledge
of habitable and fertile land around it, but only on the
north and west; the other shores are mostly wild and
unapproachable. The colour of the soil in the low lying
land is constantly changing—yellow, orange, magenta—
according to the mineral oxides present. Flocks of sheep
and especially goat are everywhere on the island; their
wilder cousins cling to precipices and call from outcrop
to outcrop in the often utter silence of the mountain.

The island offers few of the comforts of sophisticated
tourism; but the walker, climber, naturalist or poet could
ask for little more from a small Aegean island.

HISTORY

Samothrace has always derived importance from its position as a strategic refuge and landmark on the busy and very ancient maritime trade routes of the Northern Aegean. Inhabited since the Neolithic and Bronze Ages, it was first occupied by people of Thracian stock. The non-Greek Thracian language and religion survived the arrival of Greek colonists around 700 BC and were used in cult ritual as late as the 1st century BC. Archaeological evidence contradicts the Classical tradition that the colonists came from Samos before that date; Strabo suggests that the Samians invented the story for their own glory. The colonists' language has been shown by inscriptions to have been Aeolian rather than Ionian, and probably derived from Lesbos or the Troad. Homer appears familiar with the island, and in the *Iliad* (XIII, 12) envisages Poseidon watching the fighting on the plains of Troy from the 'topmost peak of forested Samothrace'. A legend relates that Troy was supposedly founded from the island, though it now seems more likely that it was from Lemnos.

In the 6th century BC Samothrace had a silver coinage, the city reached its greatest extent and colonies were established on the mainland opposite. The Samothracian navy was represented at the Battle of Salamis, fighting on the Persian side. In the 5th century BC the island's power declined, though the fame of its cult increased until the island became the chief centre of religious life in the North Aegean. Herodotus and Lysander of Sparta were initiated at the sanctuary of the Great Gods; Aristophanes and Plato refer to its 'Mysteries'; and Philip of Macedon met and fell in love with his wife Olympias of Epirus, mother of Alexander the Great, at the sanctuary. Aristarchus, commentator and editor of Homer, and head of the Library of Alexandria around 153 BC, was also a native of the island.

Samothrace was used as a naval base by the Second Athenian League, by King Lysimachos of Thrace and by the Ptolemies, Seleucids and Macedonians in turn. The island was formally incorporated into the Macedonian kingdom in 340 BC, and the dynasty continued to adorn the sanctuary until their downfall. After the Battle of Pydna in 168 BC, Perseus, the last king of Macedon sought refuge on the island only to be taken prisoner by the Romans.

The belief that Dardanos, the legendary founder of Troy, had come from Samothrace and that his descendant, Aeneas, had brought its cults to Rome gave the island a particular interest to the Romans. Varro and the statesman and collector, Lucius Calpurnius Piso (father-in-law to Julius Caesar), were initiates. Hadrian also visited Samothrace in 123 AD. St Paul appears to have stopped on the island on his way to Neapolis (Kavala) and Philippi (Acts 16.11) in 49/50 AD. A severe earthquake in c. 200 AD began the sanctuary's decline, although the ancient religion survived remarkably into the 4th century.

In 1431 the island was ceded by John VIII of Byzantium to Palamedes Gattilusi of Genoa, whose descendants styled themselves 'Princes of Ainos and Samothrace'. In 1419 the island was visited by Cristoforo Buondelmonti, and in 1444 by Cyriac of Ancona who has left posterity a couple of valuable sketches from his visit. Samothrace was taken by the Turks in 1457 who moved the inhabitants to Istanbul, and it remained an Ottoman possession (with the exception of brief occupations by the Venetians between 1466-70 and by the Russians between 1770–74), until it was liberated by the Greek fleet under Admiral Koundouriotis in 1912.

The discovery of the 'Victory of Samothrace' by the French Consul, Champoiseau, in 1863 reignited scholarly interest in the island and pulled it back from obscurity. The Sanctuary of the Great Gods was partially examined by French and Austrian archaeologists in the 1860s and 70s respectively; but the systematic uncovering of the site has mostly been the work of an American expedition (organised from New York University) which began its work in 1938 and has excavated continuously since then, with only a brief interruption during the Second World War, when the island was under a repressive Bulgarian occupation. The island received a large émigré influx from Asia Minor between the wars: the population has fallen to 2,700 today from a recorded 4,258 in 1951.

The guide to the island has been divided into three sections:
- *Chora and the south of the island*
- *The Sanctuary of the Great Gods and ancient Samothrace*
- *The north coast of the island*

CHORA &
THE SOUTH OF THE ISLAND

THE PORT AREA

Samothrace has no good, naturally sheltered, harbour anywhere on its perimeter; the few inlets offering refuge that were used in antiquity have since filled with sand and shingle. Nor is sailing always easy in the vicinity of the island: the vast and impending mass of Mount Saos creates strange and unpredictable avalanches of wind that can tumble off the mountain at any time of day or season, throwing the waters around the island into confusion. Homer placed Poseidon alone on this summit, watching the events of the Trojan War unfold; his presence here is still felt in the capricious phenomena of the sea and the winds. The modern port of **Kamariótissa** occupies the site of the ancient landing-place of *Demetrion*, and has only recently been made practicable year-round by the construction of a breakwater affording protection from the prevailing north winds. The former name, 'Demetrion', may derive from the fact that the undulating plain that stretches two or three kilometres to its east and southeast is the principal granary of the island—a gentle

and fertile area where cereals are cultivated. These beautiful fields are scattered with grazing horses and solitary
spreading oak trees—in some seasons resembling uncannily a landscape by Stubbs or Gainsborough. At the time
of the renovation of the port's principal church of the
Panaghia in 1938, the remains of a late 5th century basilica were found beneath. According to the Book of *Acts*
(16.11), St Paul put in at Samothrace overnight on his
way to *Neapolis* (Kavala) in 49 or 50 AD.

A long spit of land has formed due west of Kamariótissa, culminating in **Akrotiri point**. Against its southern
side, a small marsh area has formed which is frequented
by waders and shore-birds in periods of migration. At the
southern tip of this marsh is the small, hidden church of
Aghios Andreas, accessible by an easy walk (2km from
the port) by following the track which cuts south across
the promontory. Its west front incorporates, in haphazard
manner, several **marble elements** from an **Early Christian** *templon* screen. The church consists of a single, barrel-vaulted aisle, with a broad apse set somewhat askew.
This apse belongs to a mediaeval church on this site,
whereas the rest of the church was built in the 1870s. To
the north and east of the present church, vestigial remains
can be seen of an earlier church, perhaps the *catholicon*
of a monastery surrounded by some humble monastery

buildings. In two areas to the east of here, scattered remains of late Hellenistic settlements which were occupied through into the early Christian period have come to light.

Samothráki Chora

The **island's capital** is a beautiful example of an undisturbed and unselfconscious island *'chora'*, occupying a protected position in a natural hollow of the mountain: it is deliberately well-hidden from all sides, but nonetheless has a fine view to the sea and towards the sunset. Situated 5km to the east and inland of the port, it comes into view only at the last moment—a benign mixture of stone and wood-frame houses, mostly of the 19th century, with façades that are alternately un-rendered or whitewashed with plain or brightly coloured plaster. The town has an abundant water-supply and pleasing vegetation.

To the north, on the summit of a sheer cliff, the ruined mediaeval fortress, or **kastro**, stands above everything else—well-sited but modest in dimensions. There are two periods of construction here: the round tower to the east has the characteristic triple courses of brick tiles between the stone-work which indicate that it is of Byzantine construction and is a remnant of the 11th century fortifications. These pre-existing structures were then later much enlarged in the 15th century fortress created by the Gattilusi. A modern concrete building housing the local police has been raised inappropriately just next to the gate, but the steps up to it permit closer inspection of the tower's carved dedicatory marble plaque of 1433 commemorating in Greek its construction by the 'great, noble and patriotic, Palamedes Gattilusi', and bearing the heraldic emblems (familiar from the Castle of Mytilene) of eagles with single-head (Genoa), and double-head (Constantinople), the Palaeologus monogram, and the Gattilusi escutcheon. A second inscribed plaque, dated two years earlier and with similar elements, can be seen in the wall of the rectangular tower to the south of the entrance.

The **church of the Dormition** (1875) dominates the heart of the Chora by its imposing mass. The almost square interior is preceded by an airy narthex of large dimensions. On the south side of the nave is the golden reliquary of the Five 'Neo-martyrs' of Thrace. Originally taken hostage by the Turks in 1821 and forcibly converted to Islam, these five Samothracians re-converted to Christianity when they were returned in 1835 and later died for their faith in Makri, in Thrace.

Directly below the west front of the church, in the restored Asdránia House, is the **Municipal Folklore Museum** (*open daily June–Oct 10–1, 6–9*), laid out over two floors. The lower floor is given over to domestic artefacts, woven rugs, examples of popular *naïf* painting, and the library of the Samothracian scholar Nikolaos Phardys (1855–1901); the upper floor is dominated by a magnificent **wooden *misantra*** (a large, all-purpose dresser) constructed with few true right-angles, and a collection of fine and unusual embroidered frames for photographs.

Prehistoric Samothrace

Chora occupies the hollow to the north side of the watershed between the Katsamvás and Polypoúdi torrents: the peak of Aghios Giorgios rises steeply to its east; to the west is the knob-like **hill of Vrichós**, site of a prehistoric acropolis of the 11th century BC. The crest of the hill is marked, most conspicuously to the north, by the vestiges of an elongated circuit of megalithic walls consisting in parts of a double curtain of irregular boulders, in-filled with rubble. On the north slope below, three early Iron Age megalithic tombs have been identified.

The road south out of Chora descends to the coast through the area known as Alónia ('threshing floors') where the produce of the island's fertile western flank was processed in mills driven by the water of the Polypoúdi stream. A track parallel to its course to the west passes beside the church of Aghios Giorgios and leads to the mouth of the watercourse at the shore. Here, at **Mikró Vouní**, the island's oldest settlement of the Neolithic and Bronze Ages occupied the top of the mound just north of what would have been a small natural harbour. Evidence of an earliest phase of settlement dating from the end of the 6th millennium BC has been uncovered; by the 3rd millennium BC a typical, Aegean, proto-urban community of around 500 individuals had formed. Amongst the finds from the site are a number of Minoan clay tablets of the 19th or 18th century BC, providing important evidence of the extent of Cretan trade in metals in the area.

THE CENTRAL SOUTH COAST

Sunny, rock-strewn, dotted with sinewy, tenacious vegetation and backed by the varying colours of the mass of the mountain, the beautiful south coast of Samothrace feels like a different world from the north coast. Its outlook is no longer Thracian, but Aegean. Its minimal areas of habitation are all concentrated, in the watered valley of the Xeropótamos stream, and between the villages of Lákkoma (9km from Kamariotissa; 100m a.s.l.) and Prophítis Elías (400m a.s.l.). The **Xeropótamos valley** is given over to olive cultivation; one of the large, early-20th century waterwheels for powering the olive-mills can still be seen *in situ*. **Lákkoma** is a settlement with many old stone houses of a typically Thracian style; the lower part of the village centres on the grandly built, and now ruined, Chanos family olive mill—its windows handsomely picked out in frames of a magenta-coloured, trachytic stone. The water chute is clearly visible and much of the machinery is still in place in the interior.

From the village a road climbs (2.5km) circuitously up to the panoramic settlement of **Prophitis Elias**, in a dense patch of green on the rocky mountainside. A quarter of a kilometre before entering the village, a track leads up the hillside to the left and west, eventually heading due north (2km) to the lonely site of the chapel of **Mandál' Panaghiá**, standing beside a spring shaded by lofty plane-trees. In the area below and west of the chapel a large quantity of finds, predominantly of female figurines in marble, has indicated the presence of an early Archaic sanctuary to a Mother Goddess, which continued to flourish into late Hellenistic times, and which was later covered by Early Christian, and subsequently Byzantine, places of worship. The site is magnificently panoramic. A hard climb of a further 400m in altitude, east from the chapel, leads up to the spring of Sphendámi.

At 14.5km from Kamariotissa (5km from Lákkoma), a tortuous track climbs (left) to the Panaghía Kremniótissa—a simple, late 19th century chapel perched on a precipice above the bay of Pachiá Ammos, affording marvellous views to the west. Well above it to the east, on a plateau of the long shoulder of the mountain, are traces of an Iron Age settlement, referred to as 'Porta', overlooking the Vátos gorge below. The road ends (17km) at **Pachiá Ammos**—a fine, secluded beach of long-grain, golden sand, with a single fish-taverna. Further to the east, the mountainside drops in eight hundred metre cliffs sheer into the sea, with rock-faces riven in places by waterfalls.

THE SANCTUARY OF THE GREAT GODS & ANCIENT *SAMOTHRACE*

Due north of Chora on the coast, 5.5km from Kamari-ótissa, is the entrance to the island's principal archaeo-logical area: a signed pathway climbs for 300m up from the shoreline road, past the church of Aghia Paraskeví at the foot of a small gorge. Little other than the ruins of the walls of the actual city of **Ancient *Samothrace***, now re-ferred to as '**Palaiopolis**', remain in comprehensible con-dition; but adjacent to it, to the west, is one of the most significant sacred sites of the ancient Greek world, dedi-cated to the cult of a group of deities of early Anatolian origin, and known as the *****Sanctuary of the 'Great Gods'**. Together with the sanctuary at Eleusis in Attica, this was home to the oldest and most important of the Greek 'mystery cults': these were belief-systems or cults which involved personal initiation into certain secret revela-tions. Our knowledge of these cults is inevitably limited since those ancient writers who had been initiated, such as Herodotus and Varro, were understandably reticent to talk about them because of the consequences implicit in revealing the 'mysteries'. This means that we are far from having a clear understanding of the exact purpose of eve-

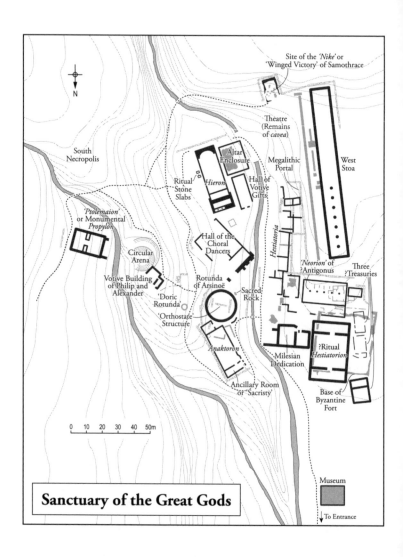

Site of the *'Nike'* or *'Winged Victory'* of Samothrace

Theatre (Remains of *cavea*)

South Necropolis

Altar Enclosure

Megalithic Portal

West Stoa

Ritual Stone Slabs

Hieron

Hall of Votive Gifts

'Ptolemaion' or *Monumental Propylon*

Circular Arena

Hall of the Choral Dancers

Hestiatoria

'Neorion' of ?Antigonus

Three ?Treasuries

Votive Building of Philip and Alexander

'Doric Rotunda'

Rotunda of Arsinoë

Sacred Rock

'Orthostate' Structure

Anaktoron

Milesian Dedication

?Ritual *Hestiatorion*

Ancillary Room or 'Sacristy'

Base of Byzantine Fort

0 10 20 30 40 50m

Sanctuary of the Great Gods

Museum

↓To Entrance

ry building that composed the sanctuary. Any visit to the site is likely to raise a number of queries that cannot easily be answered.

(*Open daily, except Mon. Site 8.30–8.30 in summer, 8.30–3.30 in winter; museum: 8.30–3.*)

Introduction

The site is dramatic, occupying a series of folds or ravines in the lower slopes of the prominent, northwest shoulder of the Saos massif. It looks north out to sea towards the Thracian coast; the summit of Aghios Giorgios (1,455m) towers directly above. In its steep and rocky setting, the site is more reminiscent of Delphi than any of the other Greek sanctuaries. In earliest times the sanctuary was entered from the hill to the west; in the 3rd century BC Ptolemy II Philadelphus created a new monumental access from the east—the side of the town. Today, however, the usual access is directly from the north, passing first by the museum building: this means that we lose the element of surprise that the ancients had, who came upon the sacred centre of the sanctuary hidden in a hollow, after the preparation of a calibrated arrival through a monumental entrance and ritual area. Both town and sanctuary were badly affected by earthquakes in the area of the Dardanelles in 287 BC, 50 AD, and—most catastrophically—around 200 AD: each time buildings were rebuilt or replaced. This means that, despite the antiquity of the cult and the sanctuary, much of the character of its buildings and lay-out is Hellenistic, dating from the period when the royal house of Macedon embellished the site and cultivated it as an important jewel in their territorial crown. The young Philip of Macedon is said to have first caught sight of the princess Olympias on the occasion of his initiation at Samothrace and to have fallen in love with her at first sight: their marriage gave birth to Alexander the Great. By the end of the 1st century BC the sanctuary must have been of considerable splendour both in sculpture and architecture. After 400 AD there was a steady process of destruction, natural and human. What is seen today is mostly the result of excavation and what stands above ground-level has been re-erected by archaeologists. Notwithstanding, the site is extensive and intriguing, and its wild setting among rocks, ravines and oak trees, with the mountain ever-present above, is unforgettable.

The discovery and subsequent removal of the famous 'Victory of Samothrace' trophy by Charles Champoiseau, the French Vice-consul in Adrianople (modern Edirne) in 1863 excited the imagination of European classicists and antiquarians. The eventual display of the sculpture on the landing of the monumental *Escalier Daru* in the Louvre in Paris was a master-stroke, and went some way to evoke the piece's original, dramatic position (*see below*). A French archaeological mission was the first to map the sanctuary; Austrian expeditions in 1873 and 1875 uncovered the *Ptolemaion*; a Swedish team worked on the site in 1923–25; but only in 1938 was systematic exploration begun by the University of New York under the direction of Karl and Phyllis Lehmann, resulting also in their excellent description of the site first published in 1954. Their work continues currently under James R. McCredie. A number of the finds made in the 19th century are divided between the archaeological collections in Paris, Vienna and Istanbul.

The historian Diodorus Siculus suggests that a cult of the Great Mother Goddess was first brought to the island by Myrina, the fearsome Queen of the Amazons (*Bibliotheke*, III. 55): 'she also gave the island the name of Samothrace which means when translated into Greek, "sacred island". The Mother of Gods was well pleased with the island', he continues, and 'she established the mysteries which are now celebrated [there]… and ordained by law that the sacred area should enjoy the right of sanctuary'. Throughout later history, the sanctuary continued to possess the extra-territorial character customarily accorded to sacred sites; it appears to have been separate from the city-state that adjoined it since it sent its own envoys, independent of the city, to the various important festivals in other parts of Greece. Its remarkable openness attracted pilgrims and aspiring initiates from a wide portion of the Mediterranean and Euxine area: contrary to the practice at Eleusis, attendance here was open to anyone, initiated or not, and initiation itself could not only be obtained at any time, but was also unusually democratic in nature making no distinction according to sex, age, social status or nationality. There appear to have been two degrees of initiation, termed '*myesis*' and '*epopteia*' which could, furthermore, be taken without an intervening interval. A certain moral standard seems to have been implicit in the second degree and some form of confession and absolution may have preceded it. The second degree of initiation was not obligatory, but rather the exception. Initiates wore a finger-ring of iron and carried a purple scarf on their person as badge of their status. The iron may have been of local origin.

On Samothrace—as in Lemnos and at Thebes in Boeotia—the cult of the Great Gods has been linked traditionally to deities called 'Cabeiri' (Strabo, *Geog.* X.3.20). Their name may derive from the Semitic root 'kabir', meaning a 'lord' or 'almighty', and have come into the Greek world through the agency of the Phoenicians, suggesting that 'Cabeiri', or 'almighty ones', may just be another name for the Great Gods. Alternatively the word may derive from the Sumerian '*cabar*', meaning 'copper'. Since there is no clear epigraphic reference to the name 'Cabeiri' at the sanctuary, we do not necessarily need to consider them as separate from the Great Gods. They may have become associated with the island in the Greek mind, by conflation, as protectors of sea voyages as they were in Phoenician mythology: Samothrace could after all only be visited by making an often difficult journey through the island's famously unpredictable waters.

THE NATURE OF MYSTERY CULTS

It is not known at what point in evolution human beings first became aware of the inevitability of death—a consciousness which appears to separate us from the rest of living creation: but once it had happened it urgently became necessary to find a way of reconciling the meaning of existence with such an uncomfortable awareness. The Olympian cults, the poets and even the philosophers of Ancient Greece are notoriously silent on the subject of the afterlife: Hades, god of the dead and of the Underworld, was for the Greeks a divinity mostly without temple or cult. He was best not mentioned. It was to fill this gap and to satisfy the deeply felt human need to 'conquer

death' that the mystery cults such as those practiced
in Samothrace and Eleusis evolved. They long pre-
date the Greek world; in fact their earliest origins
may lie in prehistoric nocturnal festivals for the exor-
cism of death. And it was perhaps for this reason that
it was most significantly at night that the Sanctuary
of the Great Gods came to life.

The fact that the forces and divinities venerated
both in Samothrace and at Eleusis, were later associated in the Greek mind with Hades, Demeter and
Persephone, and the cycles of natural regeneration,
implies that the revelations of the cult were related
to a similar concept of overcoming a fear of death
by a hope of rebirth. At Samothrace, however, the
Earth Mother, Axieros, and the Hades/Demeter pair,
Axiokersos and Axiokersa, are also accompanied by
the ithyphallic Cadmilos, the spouse of the Earth
Mother, who was later identified with the Olympian
Hermes. Sexual generation, as expressed in the erect
phallus was evidently a crucial part of the vision
that the cult offered. Herodotus, in fact, confirms as
much: in the *Histories*, Book II. 51, he explains that
the origins of nearly all Greek religious practices

were Egyptian—except, he says, the Greek custom of portraying Hermes with erect phallus, which he claims was of 'Pelasgian' origin.

> *'Anyone will understand what I mean if he is familiar with the mysteries of the Cabeiri—rites which the Samo-thracians learned from the Pelasgians, who lived in that island before they moved to Attica, and communicated the mysteries to the Athenians. This is shown by the fact that the Athenians were the first Greeks to make statues of Hermes with erect phallus, and that they learned the practice from the Pelasgians, who explained it by a certain religious doctrine, the nature of which is made clear in the Samothracian mysteries.'*

To be able to speak with such authority ('... those familiar with the mysteries' etc.), it seems likely that Herodotus was himself initiated into these mysteries, implying that it was perfectly natural for someone of his immense learning, intelligence and objectivity to go through such initiation rites.

Herodotus also refers to the mysteries as making certain things clear. In English we are ill-served by the associations of the word 'mystery', which are with opacity and incomprehension. The Greek words '*myesis*' and '*mystes*' refer simply to teaching and initiation, or the joining of a select group: they have no link with 'incomprehension'. So there is no irony or inconsistency in Herodotus's claim that the Samothracian mysteries made certain things 'clear'. As to what it was that the mysteries made clear, the following hypothesis may serve as a point of departure.

The names of the 'Great Gods' (listed in only one late, Hellenistic source)—Axieros, Axiokersos and Axiokersa—are clearly cognate variations of the same root. Like a trinity which is three in one and one in three, they are probably three aspects or embodiments of the same abiding principle—different facets of the Earth-Mother divinity, who manifests herself in the dying and regeneration of the year's cycles, in the decay and corruption of the fruit which symbolises her and which in turn engenders and feeds the seeds within to form new life. This makes her always regenerating and yet eternally static and the same. She is a trinity of birth, death and perpetuity. But this eternal cycle can only be set in motion or given worldly actuality by her partner, Cadmilos, who is characterised principally by his erect phallus—the transmitter of new seed. He has been created separate from her, but by his yearning to be united with her completes and perpetuates the cycle of replenishment, himself 'dying' in every intercourse only to ensure the generation of new life. The vision that this affords, first of all, is one of birth and death being aspects of the same phenomenon, implying that death should not therefore be feared as an irremediable termination. But it also implies that the perpetuation of life through the seed, the perpetuation of the group or the species—the process, that is—is more important than the survival of the individual ego. As Herodotus implies the cult was very ancient; it harked back to an age before the full evolution of the human sense of ego which came with the philosophical and political revolutions of 6th and 5th century BC Greece. The mysteries, therefore, may have aimed to help the initiate to conquer the anxiety of individual survival by looking beyond to the more universal patterns of human regeneration.

It is impossible to reconstruct how all this might

have been communicated in the spaces which have so far been uncovered by the archaeologists. But the analogy of a Christian liturgy would not be out of place. An Orthodox or Catholic mass involves the ritual acting out of religious truths, the repetition of formulae, the wearing of special costumes (by the priests), the showing of symbolic objects, and the participation in a ritual eating and drinking—all of which to the 'uninitiated' can seem either moving, or mystifying, or merely bogus. Archaeological finds, such as ritual bowls and lamps for every participant, spaces possibly used for changing clothes, sacred symbols and rings symbolising fellowship, suggest that all the eucharistic elements mentioned above had counterparts in the enacting of the 'mysteries'. We simply lack the sacred narrative that linked them into a coherent 'liturgy'.

The museum

The path from the entrance leads first to the small **museum** (200m) before entering the archaeological site. (*Note: the museum closes at 3 pm throughout the year.*)

The **Central Hall (A)**, entered first, is dedicated to architectural fragments. The prevailing taste and period is that of the High Hellenistic Age (4th–2nd centuries BC), with emphasis on an elegant and ornate decoration. To the right stands a reconstructed segment of the upper portion or 'gallery' of the great **Rotunda of Arsinoë** (c. 285 BC), its graceful curve bound by the low frieze of garlanded *bucrania* and rosettes, rhythmically alternating blank space with clear and concise decoration. The surface of the stone is beautifully hand-worked with a mason's point. To its right, in the corner, is part of its elegant, laurel-decorated roof-finial; to the left, a small segment of the roof and eaves, illustrates the complexity of the tile designs necessary for a conical roof. At the opposite end of the hall are elements from the entablature and roof of the *Hieron*, including fragments (southeast corner) from the *acroterion* which surmounted its pediment—a piece of intricate decorative fantasy, impressively reconstructed in a model above the doorway into *Hall B*. The highly skilled drill-work and virtuoso quality of much of the marble decoration is typical of the production of the sculptural workshops in such centres as Aphrodisias in Asia Minor during this period (mid-2nd century BC): the marble, however, is almost certainly Thasian.

Hall B (to the south) is dominated by the reconstruction of the impressive

Corinthian capital and base from the *Propylaia* of Ptolemy II (285–281 BC)—reminiscent in its clarity of the capital executed by Polycleitus the Younger for the *Thymele* at Epidaurus. In the corner by the entrance is also a fluted, monolithic column in Thasian marble from the 'Hall of the Choral Dancers', surmounted by a beautiful 'collar' decorated with palmettes, giving it a vividly oriental, Ionic feel. Beside it is a section of the frieze of the same building showing a gracious *****processional dance of women**—regular and rhythmic, but never mechanically repetitive. The deliberately archaising dress and head-gear they wear contrasts pleasingly with the Hellenistic naturalism of their movement. The

work was executed around 340 BC possibly by the school of Scopas. The sculptures in Thasian marble on the other side of the doorway—a **bust of the blind seer, Teiresias**, and a headless figure of Persephone—are considerably eroded; they had lain in the bed of the stream to the east of the museum for several centuries and may have been part of the pediment tableau of an earlier mid-5th century BC building in the sanctuary. (The Teiresias bust was seen and drawn in 1444 by the Italian antiquarian, Cyriac of Ancona, who believed it to be a portrait of Aristotle; the piece was later mounted in the façade of a house in Chora as a protective talisman up until its removal in the last century.) Around the walls of the room are show-cases exhibiting small finds from the site—a variety of portable altars, eroded effigies and figurines, coins, offerings and inscriptions. A fineness of decoration prevails through-out—as in the delicately sculpted lids from the cof-fered ceiling of the entrance to the hall of Choral Dancers (*case on rear wall*). To the left, in the corner, are two interest-ing *stelai*, both dedicated on Samothrace by initiates resi-dent in the city of *Cyzicus* on the Sea of Marmara, and both depicting the entrance to a circular building reminiscent of the Rotunda of Arsinoë: the more fragmentary of the two was again meticulously drawn by Cyriac of Ancona in 1444 (drawing in Bodleian Library, Oxford).

Hall C. Two pieces dis-played in the centre of the hall are of particular beauty: in the centre of the room is an elegantly **carved bench-support** with a graceful, inverted bluebell motif, which came from the area of the Hall of the Choral Dancers. Beyond is a large **Nike statue** in marble (c. 130 BC) which was the corner *acroterion* of the roof of the *Hieron*—one of four similar figures which would have marked all four corners of the building. From her (missing) right arm she would have poured a libation into a shallow *patera* held in her outstretched left hand. Beautifully executed, with masterful running-drill work in the drapery in particular, her poise and movement belong to a late, Hellenistic culture very different from the archaic and protean world from which the cult itself of the Great Gods emerged. Behind and to the left, *case no. 7* exhibits fragments from a number of magnificent, 6th and 5th century BC, **painted column craters**—funerary monuments, principally from excavations in the area of the necropolis. Many are of Attic origin, occasionally signed by the artist: the painting is of the highest quality. The numerous show cases in the room display a wide array of ceramics and of small devotional, ornamental and funerary objects. *Cases no. 9 & no. 10* exhibit a variety of interesting glassware, often of a type with striped design, fired on a sand-core.

The Byzantine ceramics in *case no. 12*, give evidence of the continuity of habitation in the area.

To the north side of **Hall A**, is **Hall D**, whose entrance affords, looking back, a good view of the beautiful design of the interior of the reconstructed fragment of the Rotunda of Arsinoë, and of the running friezes and delicate Corinthian capitals of the columns which contitute its decoration. A cast of the '*Victory of Samothrace*' trophy (*see pp. 128–129*), now in the Louvre in Paris, stands in the northeast corner of the room. The show-cases display finds mostly from graves in the area. To the left are notable examples of plain and deco-rated Archaic ceramics; to the right, much fine, Hellenistic **jewellery** and exquisite **figu-**

rines, whose delicacy when originally coloured would have been even greater.

The central sacred area

As you ascend the hidden ravine in the fold of the foothills towards the site, many of the fragments of marble to left and right are very eroded because they were retrieved from the stream-bed below; others, left above ground, have suffered the milder erosion of the wind.

To the left, across the stream bed, is the colossal base (20.2m in outside diameter) of the *****Rotunda of Arsinoë**—once the greatest of the circular buildings of Greek antiquity—dedicated to the Great Gods by Queen Arsinoë II, wife successively of Lysimachus of Thrace and of her own brother, Ptolemy II 'Philadelphus'. It was probably begun after extensive damage was wrought on the preexisting buildings by the earthquake of 287 BC. Built on a site historically dedicated to sacred libations and sacrifices, the rotunda must have continued this function, as well as serving as a focus for the solemn gatherings of envoys and officials for the sanctuary's festivals. Its symbolism was important: circular buildings, such as *martyria* and baptisteries in later times, were associated in Antiquity and Early Christian practice with the union of death and new life, one of the central themes of the Samothracian cult. The exterior presented a marble wall surmounted by an ornamental string-course, below a gallery of pilasters supporting a Doric entablature; the dark and spacious interior was vaulted with a low conical roof on a wooden armature. Since much of the sanctuary's ritual occurred at night by torch-light, there was no need for windows. What we see today is the vast ring of limestone foundations, surmounted by the steps in Thasian marble of the superstructure which formerly rose nearly 13m above.

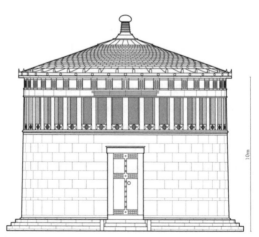

10m

The Rotunda of Arsinoë (c. 280BC): elevation of the building, after the reconstruction drawn by John Kurtich.

In the centre of the rotunda (at a level once well beneath its floor) archaeologists have revealed the rectangular plan of the southern end of the early 4th century BC predecessor of the '*anaktoron*', referred to as the '**orthostate structure**'. Much more ancient and of primary ritual importance, immediately to the southwest of the perimeter of the rotunda, is the **Sacred Rock**—a small, natural outcropping of blue-green porphyritic rock separated by a narrow channel from a surrounding pavement of yellow-brown tuff. The pouring of sacred libations on outcrops of coloured rock has a history which goes back far in time and was a fundamental element in all varieties of Mother-goddess worship in Anatolia. More highly polished examples of this kind of coloured, sacred rock can be seen at the important Hittite cultic centres in Turkey such as at Boğazkale.

The central hall for the first degree of initiation into the Mysteries, referred to traditionally as the '*Anaktoron*' (meaning a 'princely' or 'divine residence') stretches to the northwest a little below the rotunda, cut partially into the slope of the hill: its rectangular plan of ashlar walls in polygonal limestone blocks is well-preserved to a considerable height. As a very sacred and ancient building, it was always rebuilt in the same manner when damaged; the present structure is faithful to its predecessors although

it dates from the 1st century AD. The spacious, probably
window-less, interior (27m x 11.5m) was entered from
the long west side by three doors whose thresholds still
remain. The roof beams were supported by the pilasters
whose bases can be seen on the wall opposite, along which
appears to have stretched a grandstand of low seats, facing a central, circular wooden platform. A wooden parti-
tion wall with doors—perhaps not dissimilar to a church
iconostasis—raised on a low wall distinguished by a layer
of red, porphyry-like stone, separated a zone at the north
end: this appears to have been an **inner sanctuary**, whose
entrances were marked by bronze statues and a *stele* (now
in the museum, *Hall A*) forbidding entry by the uninitiated. At the opposite, south end of the building is a small
ancillary room, designated a '**sacristy**'. Marble slabs re-
cording initiations appear to have been immured here in
the walls above low, stone benches.

The *Anaktoron* and the Rotunda define a central north/
south axis of the sanctuary along the ridge: further to the
south along this axis are found the other holy buildings
of the sanctuary.

Of the 4th century BC marble building which lies to the
south of the Rotunda—known as the '**Hall of the Choral Dancers**' after the beautiful frieze of female dancers
which adorned its entablature (museum, *Hall B*)—little

remains standing. Elements from it preserved in the museum show that the building was remarkable for the fineness and variety of its decoration; the coffers of its ceiling were carved with beautiful heads and faces, its monolithic columns embellished with delicately patterned collars, and it may have housed the famous group depicting *Aphrodite and Pothos* by Scopas, which is mentioned by Pliny (*Nat. Hist.* XXXVI. 25). Indeed, Karl Lehmann suggests that Scopas may have been the presiding designer of the building. The pedimented portico of the building would have been clearly visible out to sea.

Just to the south, at the heart of the sanctuary, are the re-erected Doric columns of the **Hieron** ('sacred building')—a long rectangular, colonnaded structure which terminated in an apse at its south end, having much the appearance internally of a basilica. This was the place of initiation of the second and higher degree—of the '*epopteia*'. The building's roof-line, punctuated by the elaborate antefixes and *acroteria* which are now in the museum, and marked at the corners by the four beautiful winged victory-figures, must have been singularly impressive. The interior, once again was windowless and roofed with a wooden, coffered ceiling: its walls were painted black and red and must have appeared solemn by torch light. Along the east and west walls were low stone benches with carved supports, and at the centre of the apsidal area—in the position corresponding to the altar in a Christian basilica—was a libation pit. Entry to the interior was explicitly forbidden by an inscribed *stele* to noninitiates of the second degree. The aspiring *epoptes* may have had to undergo some sacred preparation standing on the stone slabs, framed with terracotta tiles, which are still visible in the ground outside the building, half way down the east side (now protected by glass) beside the stylobate of the building. Lehmann suggests that priest and *mystes* faced one another here across a stone in the middle into which a torch was fixed to exchange a confession and absolution; but the interpretation remains purely conjectural.

The existing building was begun in c. 325 BC, was only finished in the middle of the 2nd century BC, and underwent several later restorations in antiquity. It, in turn, replaced earlier buildings—always with an apse—dating from the 6th and 5th centuries BC respectively. Today we see only its eroded, limestone core, inside a fine shell of Thasian marble in places. Five columns of the double porch were re-erected in 1956: the pedimental statuary is in Vienna.

As you walk south down the east side of the *Hieron*, directly ahead of you in the polygonal limestone wall is a boss with a faint cross carved on its surface. On the opposite, west side of the building is the main **altar enclosure**—a large, boxed-in structure, yet open to the skies so that the gods above could also be witness to the offerings. Fragments of the architrave bear a dedicatory inscription of (?)Arrhidaios, the half-brother of Alexander the Great. The building was entered from the west and any orands would have faced east. Next to the altar building, to the north is one of the oldest surviving structures of the sanctuary the so-called '**Hall of Votive Gifts**', built originally around 540 BC, and subsequently only minimally modified. Normally votive gifts and offerings were stored in the *naos* or *opisthodomos* of a temple; but here, because of the liturgical function of the interior of the *Hieron*, they needed to be stored from earliest times, in a separate building.

Facing these two last buildings from the west is the *cavea* of the small **theatre**, fashioned from a declivity in the hillside and looking over the most sacred area of the sanctuary. Rising conspicuously above the southern extremity of the *cavea*, on the crown of the ridge, once soared the sculptural complex we know as the *Nike* or '*Winged Victory of Samothrace*', which now dominates the grand Escalier Daru of the Louvre in Paris. The amorphous rubble of the open-fronted, rectangular terrace where it once stood—originally conceived to create the impression of billowing water through which the ship's prow, on which the *Nike* hovered, made headway—is all that remains to be seen on site. The sculpture was raised high above the ground on the carved prow, leaving the gilded palm frond or wreath—which some suggest she may have held in her outstretched arm—to catch the light.

THE NIKE OF SAMOTHRACE

Few pieces in all of Hellenistic sculpture use the swinging counterpoint of drapery as effectively and dramatically as the *Nike* of Samothrace. The divinity of intoxicating victory alights auspiciously on the prow of a military vessel with her drapery pressed against her by the wind. In a powerful piece of virtuoso illusionism, inert and solid marble is made to hover for a moment—weightlessly. In few pieces of sculpture do drama and material identify so closely.

The *Nike* was first unearthed in 1863 by the French Vice-consul in Adrianople, Charles Champoiseau, and was taken to Paris; the pedestal in the form of a ship's prow followed 20 years later; and a fragmentary right hand, raised in greeting, which some believe held a gilded symbol of victory, was found on the site in 1950. The piece was part of an extravagant monument of Rhodian workmanship—possibly the work of Pithokritos—erected around 200 BC in the sanctuary to celebrate and give thanks for a Rhodian naval victory in the war with Antiochos. It was not uncommon for boats and trophies to be consecrated at the great sanctuaries of the Greek world in commemoration of victorious battles, and the marine connection with Samothrace was anyway strong; the sanctuary was much patronised by sailors desirous of averting shipwreck or grateful for salvation from disaster at sea. Much of the piece's effect must have depended on the original setting: the whole ensemble stood, between mountain and sea, above the heart of the sanctuary, in a pool apparently filled with water and rocks carved to appear like billows. At night, when the sanctuary was most frequented, lighting with flickering lamps may have added to the sculpture's powerful presence.

The western ridge

The ridge to the west of the main sacred area was crowned at its southern end by a magnificent *stoa* which must have dominated the sky-line, overlooked the principal sacred buildings and offered good views of the *Winged Victory* monument to its east. The building, erected in the first half of the 3rd century BC, was a sober structure with Doric columns and entablature, its limestone core faced with a marble-white stucco. In front of its long, east face stood honorific and votive statues, whose bases can still be seen; the best preserved is at the south end. The building's considerable length (c. 104m) required the natural slope to be built up at the north end. This was the main public building of the sanctuary, designed on a scale to shelter and to provide a meeting space for the increasing numbers of pilgrims and visitors.

Directly below it on the eastern face of the ridge looking across towards the *Hieron*, is an area of problematic finds. The visitor sees amongst the trees the foundations and walls of a series of buildings and terraces forming deep, right-angle corners against the steep slope of the ridge. Above are walls in fine, rectangular isodomic masonry; while below are walls of much older-looking polygonal stone work. In the corner of the latter, is a massive **lintel-block and relieving triangle** over a rectangular entrance into the hillside, looking as though it were the doorway of a Mycenaean tomb or shrine. To the left of it the polygonal masonry of the retaining wall roughly frames two massive **projections of blue-green natural rock** similar in type to the Sacred Rock observed near the Rotunda. To the right the wall is strengthened with sand-stone buttresses. Sources are silent and archaeologists reticent as to what this is and what purpose it served: Karl Lehmann implies that when the area was taken in hand in the late 3rd century BC, the wall and the portal were created intentionally with the impression of 'venerable age' in conformity with some 'Samothracian legend of the heroic age'. This is an interesting explanation: it recalls the similar nature of the '*Antron*' of Mount Kynthos on Delos (*see vol 4, pp. 97–98*), which appears also to have been constructed in a much later epoch, but in a deliberately archaising style which recalled a Bronze Age megalithic portal. It is not incompatible with the evidence, however, that the doorway and the two breaches of the blue-green 'sacred rock' in the wall may genuinely be of a substantially earlier period, and might mark the site of an area that incorporated a now defunct spring in the hillside.

The continuation north of this area, below the eastern slope of the western ridge is marked by a series of three adjacent, rectangular rooms which were probably *hesti-*

tatoria, or ritual banqueting rooms, with open porches on their eastern side looking onto the main sanctuary buildings. The marble-chip floor, probably of Imperial Roman times, is still preserved in parts. Such rooms are a common feature of sanctuaries and served for the public and priestly consumption of sacrificial offerings in honour of the deities. Just to the west of here, along the slope below the north end of the great *stoa*, is a long rectangular building in the form of a **boat-shed** or '*neorion*' for the display of a consecrated, victorious warship, dedicated possibly by the Macedonian King, Antigonus Gonatas, after his victory in the waters off *Cos* in 254 BC. The layout of the building is recognisable and a couple of seven marble supports which cradled the keel of the boat are still in place. The public viewing-aisle was along the north side. The immaculate masonry of the south wall, separated from the slope by a drainage channel, is well-preserved.

The sanctuary appears to have expanded into the large area to the north of the *neorion*, in late Hellenistic times, apparently in order to accommodate the construction of buildings dedicated by other Aegean city-states and their citizens. Ongoing archaeological work has clearly revealed the foundations of a number of distinct buildings. The two largest—in the centre and to the right—were never completed. An inscription pertaining to the eastern building indicates that it was the dedication of a rich lady from Miletus; the building may have been destined as another **ritual *hestiatorion***. Even the individual architectural elements in Thasian marble are clearly unfinished: the large block at an oblique angle in the extreme southeast corner is an example. At the western edge beyond the base of the large central unfinished building are three small buildings of the 3rd and 2nd centuries BC, whose compact form with portico would suggest they may have functioned as **treasuries** for donor city-states. Superimposed over this whole area was a large Byzantine fortress (c. 36m x 38m), added at some point in the 10th or 11th century AD.

The eastern ridge

Sanctuaries such as this, visited by people from all over the Greek world and beyond, inevitably attracted philanthropic dedications of buildings that were often of a self-serving, propagandistic nature. The skyline of the Eastern Hill was in Antiquity peopled by cenotaphs and monumental dedications of the great and powerful. Around 285 BC Ptolemy II Philadelphus created a new **monumental *Propylon***, sometimes called the '***Ptolemaion***', through which the sanctuary could now be entered from the east side, where the ancient city of Samothrace was located.

(This marks the eastern extremity of the sanctuary area and is reached by the path which climbs east from the Hieron.)

Fragments of Ptolemy's dedicatory inscription on the architrave can be seen amongst the blocks collected by the archaeologists beside the base of the building; among the fragments is an eroded corner-stone with an elegant relief of a ship on two of its sides. The impressive substructure of the *propylon* built in isodomic limestone blocks is still well-preserved; it is perforated by a **barrel-vaulted tunnel** at the foundation level, which allowed a watercourse to pass under it. In the earth-moving required for the gateway's construction, the seasonal torrent which descends from the southeast was diverted through this tunnel and returned to its natural gulley further to the north: this was so as to allow a solid ramp to fill the gulley, joining the gateway to the sanctuary to its west. At some point in the 2nd century AD, an earthquake swept this away, returning the torrent to its natural course, and leaving the gateway isolated. After this time the gulley was probably crossed by a wooden bridge. The propylon had the appearance of an amphi-prostyle temple with two pedimented porticos of six columns to front and back—Ionic to the east, Corinthian to the west. The latter constitutes the earliest known example of the Corinthian order used in an exterior portico in Greek architecture.

The *propylon* led directly across to a small **circular arena**, encircled by shallow rising steps (*reached by returning west back across the torrent gulley, and taking the path immediately to the north*). Too shallow for seats, these steps allowed people to stand and watch some as yet unidentified ritual that took place here, perhaps before proceeding into the sanctuary proper. There may well have been an altar positioned in the centre. The steps were constructed in the 5th century BC, and may have been enlarged at a later date. The circle is incomplete on the east side because of a landslip which has carried the masonry down into the gulley below; this probably occurred during the same earthquake which swept away the ramp joining the area to the *propylon* of Ptolemy and which reinstated the torrent in its natural course once again. The same fate has befallen the large rectangular building at an oblique angle to the north of the steps, a good third of which has fallen into the gulley. This was a large structure, in different kinds of marble, with a hexastyle portico in the Doric order overlooking the steps. It was a **commemorative dedication** erected **in honour of Philip III and Alexander IV** of Macedon (successors to Alexander the Great) between 323 and 317 BC. At a later date, an Ionic portico was added on its north side for the display of statues.

Following the path north through the trees down the

west side of the slope brings you to the scant remains and site of a curious building—possibly a commemorative cenotaph—which had the form of a tall, **Doric rotunda** of the mid- to late- 4th century BC. Its narrow diameter (4.1m) and considerable height (perhaps c.7m) preclude its use as a ceremonial or meeting building, and suggest that it was always intended to be an adornment to the skyline.

Ancient *Samothrace* and the Gattilusi Towers

Of the ancient settlement and city of Samothrace, which lay on the ridge of the mountain to the east of the Sanctuary, only the **walls** remain today above ground. The path which continues beyond the *Ptolemaion* to the north and east, leads directly to these. (*Exploration of them appears to be discouraged officially, but this may simply because the area is considerably overgrown and difficult to traverse in certain seasons.*) The walls constitute an enceinte of 2,400m—almost two thirds complete—which can be seen climbing up the ridge to the east to a look-out post at a height of 275m a.s.l., after which they drop steeply down the eastern side of the ridge, traceable only at intermittent points. Originally constructed in the 6th century BC, they have been repeatedly repaired, with a number of the corners and bastions clearly reinforced around the

3rd century BC. They are similar in construction to sectors of the walls of Thasos, with two parallel curtain walls in-filled with rubble. Five **gates** are still identifiable, the most interesting being just to the right of the main pathway—combining a curiously protruding protective bastion in its structure. The city is known to have had an important sanctuary of Athena, but this has not yet been located, though archaeological soundings have concentrated in their search for it at the eastern extremity of the area near the ruins of the church of Aghios Giorgios.

Clearly visible above the thick undergrowth which has buried everything else are the outcrops of three early 15th century **Genoese towers** to the northeast, known since Cyriac of Ancona saw them in 1444 as the **Gattilusi Towers**. (*These can also be reached by a path which leads up from the small parking-lot by the shore, 250m along the road to the east of the entrance to the archaeological site.*) They would appear to form a unity together, perhaps originally joined like corner bastions in a small fortress whose curtain wall has mostly collapsed. The highest and largest stands almost complete at nearly 18m, with the corbels for machicolations around its top still well preserved, although the wooden or stone parapet they supported has now gone. All three could only be entered by a door four or five metres above ground level, by means of a wooden ladder which led to a level above the blind storage and cistern area at ground level: two further wooden floors above were accessible by wooden stairs. The masonry includes many ancient blocks gathered from the city and the sanctuary: a mediaeval inscription in Greek on one in the southeast corner tells us that a certain Stroïlos was the supervising builder. It seems likely that the towers functioned more as advance lookouts than as a protective fortress for any of the local population. The Byzantine fort which stood on the western hill of the Sanctuary of the Great Gods (over the foundations of two of the 'treasuries' and the large unfinished Hellenistic structure) may have been used in conjunction with these towers for the defence of the island by the Gattilusi overlords.

Due north of the towers at the level of the shore, and inside the coast-road shortly before it deflects to the right (southeast) are the foundations of a small **Early Christian church** uncovered in 1938. It is thought that the church may have been erected many centuries later to commemorate the visit of the Apostle Paul to the island on his way to *Neapolis* (Kavala) in c. 50 AD; the stop-over on Samothrace is referred to in *Acts* 16.11. The harbour in which he would most likely have landed lies 150m to the west of the church, marked by a harbour mole still visible beneath the water when calm.

THE NORTH COAST OF THE ISLAND

Beyond the landmark of the Gattilusi Towers the coast road follows the shoreline east, passing below the villages of Kato and Ano (Epano) Karyótes. Just beyond the turning to the latter, two **ceramic workshops of the Hellenistic period** have been excavated to both sides of the modern road, revealing also a complex of several kilns beside the shore which were given over to a production of wine *amphorae* which continued into Roman Imperial times.

At 12km from Kamariótissa, a turning leads inland to the small settlement of **Thérma**, which takes its name from a group of geothermic springs in the area, and which may have been the site of a sanctuary of Asklepios in Antiquity. The village is shaded by countless plane trees fed by two plentiful streams which descend from the mountain. It has many tavernas and simple places to stay, a number of which are attractively immersed in burgeoning gardens of hydrangeas between the village and the shore. The **Municipal Thermal Baths** (*open daily June–Oct 7–11, 5–7*), which offer immersion pools at 39°C, are located in the functional building to the right of the road. By following the track uphill to the right side as you face this building, you come after fifty metres to two hotter, smaller pools on the hillside—one open to the air

(48°C), the other in an improvised hut (59.5°C). These are known as '**Psarótherma**' and are open and accessible at all times. The water is slightly saline and sulphurous. The main path for climbers up the north face of Mount Saos towards its peaks, via the **springs of Kalamíthria**, leaves from the southwest corner of Therma.

The **Saos massif**, with its gorges, forests, abundant springs and waterfalls, is an impressive wilderness to explore for the climber and naturalist, but it can also be a dangerous place because of the rapid weather changes. Appropriate precautions need to be taken and the ascent should be made in company—ideally with a guide who can be found by asking at the hotels in Therma, or with a dedicated hiking guidebook. The peaks of Phengari and Aghios Giorgios are usually approached from Therma, and either one can be reached in a little over four hours of strenuous climb, with the same or more for the descent; but the intermittent paths, even in clear weather, are not easy to follow in the upper altitudes. It is always wise to consult local knowledge first for a prognostication of the weather: a local publication, '*Samothraki, an Ecotourist and Trekking Map*', available in the shops in Kamariótissa, is also of considerable assistance. There are other tracks on the hotter, drier southern slopes leading up from Prophitis Elias, and from Panaghia Krimniótissa to the

Malakós spring and Aghia Thekla. Any days, however, spent rambling in this magnificent mountain massif will reward the explorer with some of the wildest and most impressive landscapes and views in the Aegean, as well as moments of unworldly and often disconcerting silence.

One and a half kilometres along the coast road beyond Therma (just after the Camping Ground on the left), a track leads to the south (right), passing a refuse area, and after thirty minutes of serpentine climbing comes to the ruined **monastery of Christós**, hidden in a grove of trees on a knoll and marked by a modern hut nearby. The site is abandoned and numinous. Only the ruins of the *catholicon* still stand, though the foundations and traces of the monastic buildings lie to all sides. The monastery appears to have been a 14th century foundation and may have been related to a mediaeval settlement whose remains are scattered in the area below and to the north: it was finally abandoned approximately 150 years ago. The simple vaulted nave, which curves slightly on its central axis, and the wide narthex are still standing, but roofless: traces of pictorial decoration are visible in the blind arch of the north wall. The building may have had external porticos along its long flanks indicated by the blind arcades which are still discernible. Particularly noteworthy are the massive lintel blocks of the doors in Thasian marble, bearing inscriptions listing the *Theoroi* (envoys) of the sanctuary of the Great Gods, from whence these blocks and the scattered Doric capitals must have been removed.

At a distance of 4.7km from Therma the coast road crosses the Phoniás river—the richest in water of all the streams that come down from Mount Saos. To the north of the road bridge, a path leads down the east bank of the stream to the **Phoniás Tower** which stands solitarily on the shore and must have functioned as a watchtower in a signalling chain. The tower would have been built by the Gattilusi overlords in the mid-15th century in the same period as the those at Palaiopolis: its construction in stone, bound in lime mortar with tiles, and the evidence of machicolation around the rim, are similar. Access to the entrance, 4m above ground level on the north side, was only by a removable wooden ladder. Its wooden floors are gone, but the careful arcading in the interior of the walls can still be seen.

To the south of the road bridge, paths along the edge of the **Phonias river** lead inland along a tunnel of huge plane trees. The massive, tangled roots of the trees penetrate the water, the land and the boulders to all sides. The first of several deep pools with **waterfalls** which punctuate the river's descent from the mountain through a rocky gorge, dense with vegetation, is reached after 30 minutes. The watercourse is rich in frogs, moths, dragonflies and all kinds of insect life. At several points the path passes the vestigial remains of ancient settlements beside the river—the most conspicuous being at a distance of about 500m in from the road on the east bank.

A further 400m east along the road from the bridge at Phoniás, an indistinct track leads off to the south towards a hillock crowned with trees above a deserted house, about 800m inland from the road. To the west side are the remains of the twin mediaeval churches of Aghios Konstantinos and Aghia Eleni: the decorated apses and walls still stand in places to a considerable height.

After Phoniás the landscape changes as the road turns south with good views of the island of Imroz (Ancient *Imbros*) and the Turkish coast. The lower slopes of the mountain are gentler and have favoured a scattering of small agricultural villages, mediaeval in origin and today barely inhabited, which have lived off the cultivation of fruit and nut trees, and olives pressed in local water-mills. There are the ruined remains of several early Byzantine churches in the area among whose ruins can be found Byzantine capitals and inscriptions. This group of settlements—**Isómata**, **Kantarátika**, **Remboutsádika**—has something of the remote and untouched quality of the villages of Ikaria's far west coast. The highest and south-ernmost village, **Kerasiá**, now abandoned, is immersed in forest and accessible only by foot from Kantarátika—a place of rare, dense, sylvan beauty and utter tranquillity.

The coastal road ends in the island's southeast corner at the splendid bay of **Kípi**, 27km from Kamariótissa. There is a long, wide beach in a deep cleft of the mountain, which constitutes the shore of a triangular valley, once cultivated like a *kípos* ('garden') and watered by a seasonal torrent. At this point the impenetrable cliffs of the south coast begin. The goats, which can be seen and heard everywhere around, seek to eat the shoots on the lower branches of the few trees and will climb onto vehicles parked in their shade in an attempt to reach them. A helpful sign warns drivers of this risk.

PRACTICAL INFORMATION

680 01 Samothraki: area 180 sq. km; perimeter 58km; resident population 2,712; max. altitude 1611 m. Port Authority: 25510 41305. **Travel and information**: Samothraki Municipality—www.samothraki.gr; Saos Travel, T. 25510 41411.

ACCESS

Access to Samothrace is principally from Alexandroupolis in Thrace. **Saos Ferries** provide a daily service to the island by both ferry and hydrofoil (afternoons), with a second (morning) hydrofoil in addition at weekends. There are also ferry connections to and from Lemnos (4 per week), Lesbos (3 per week), Psará (2 per week), Lavrion (for Athens) (2 per week), and Kavala (1 per week). Alexandroupolis airport is served with daily connections from Athens by *Olympic Air* and *Aegean Airlines*.

LODGING

Samothrace has few fully-fledged hotels, but many rooms and studio-apartments for rent. The slightly soulless **Hotel Kastro** at Palaiopolis (*T. 25510 89400*) is the island's newest hotel and is close to the sanctuary of the Great

Gods; **Hotel Elektra** at Therma (*T. 25510 98242*), and **Hotel Aiolos** at Kamariótissa (*T. 25510 41795, fax 41810*) are also practical solutions. But near to Therma are countless family houses with attractive gardens thronged with hydrangeas, where rooms can be rented very inexpensively, e.g. **Michail Aravis' Rooms** (*T. 25510 9841*). Just on the edge of Kamariótissa are the **Kyrkos Apartments** (*T. 25510 41620*)—clean, pleasant, spacious and practical.

EATING

In Chora, the **Café Ouzeri '1900'** in the main *plateia* is an enjoyable place to eat and is popular with locals: similarly, the **Taverna Orizontas** in Kamariótissa. **Pyrgos** by the castle in Chora is also pleasant for a sunset drink and *mezedes*. The best fare, however, with many excellent local goat dishes, is to be found at the **Taverna Karydies** in Mesa Meriá near Isómata at the east end of the island.

If you have to wait there for a ferry, **Alexandroupolis** offers many good eating places: amongst them, the **Ouzeri Alexis** (behind the 'Academy' building between the main street and the shore) deserves recommendation and has excellent fish and good service.

FURTHER READING

Karl Lehmann, *Samothrace* (Institute of Fine Arts, New York University), Thessaloniki 1998.

GLOSSARY

acroterion—an ornamental fixture on the extremity of a building

amphi-prostyle—(of a building) with an entrance or portico of free-standing columns at both ends

amphora—a tall, terracotta receptacle with handles for transportation of liquids

apotropaic—having the power to turn away evil

Archaic period—the 7th and 6th centuries BC

ashlar—stone masonry using large, dressed, regular blocks

bole—a very fine red clay, typically from Armenia ('Armenian bole')

bucranium (pl. *bucrania*)—a decorative design of skulls of oxen linked by garlands used mostly on pagan altars

catholicon—the church at the centre of an Orthodox monastery

cavea—the hemicycle of seats accommodating the public in a theatre

citharode—someone who plays or sings to the cithara or lyre

clerurchy—an imposed colony in which settlers keep the citizenship of their home city *deme*—the body politic, and (by extension) the land, of an ancient Greek township

dinos **cup**—a wide, ceramic vessel used as a mixing bowl

Euxine (**Sea**)—the ancient name for the Black Sea

Geometric period—the 10th–late 8th centuries BC

Hellenistic period—era of, and after, the campaigns of Alexander the Great, c. 330–c. 150 BC

hestiatorion—a building for ritual dining

hexastyle—(of an ancient building) with a portico of six columns

hypostyle—an architectural space with a flat roof supported on columns

iconostasis—the high wooden screen (generally holding icons and images) which separates the sanctuary from the main body of an Orthodox church, and which with time came to substitute the masonry *templon* (*see below*) of earlier Byzantine churches

isodomic—(of masonry) constructed in parallel courses of neatly-cut rectangular blocks

kantharos—a pottery drinking vessel with a deep cup and two handles which typically rise higher than the lip of the cup

machicolation—a defensive projection out from a fortified building, often over the entrance or at a corner, from which projectiles or hot liquids could be dropped on assailants

martyrion—a building (mostly circular) which enshrines the remains of a holy person, similar to, and deriving from, the pagan heroön

megaron—the great hall of a Mycenaean palace, rectangular in shape and generally preceded by a porch; an ancient building which shares this form

mihrab—the resonating and often ornate niche in the wall of a mosque which indicates the *qibla* or sacred direction of Mecca

misantra—a large wooden, open-fronted storage cupboard, similar to a dresser

naos—the central, inside chamber of a temple

Nike—the winged divinity of victory

neorion (pl. *neoria*)—(in a sanctuary) a gallery for exhibiting a boat as votive offering; (more generally) a shed for the storing and drying of wooden boats

opisthodomos—a room or storage space to the rear of the *naos* (*qv*) of a temple

Osmanli—the Ottoman Turkish language, especially when written in Arabic script

panegyri—a traditional, outdoor festival in Greece, often of religious (sometimes pagan) inspiration

patera—a shallow, saucer-like dish, for drinking or for libations *peristyle*—a colonnade which encloses an area, a building or a courtyard

pithos (pl. *pithoi*)—a large, tall, ceramic storage jar, sometimes used also for burials

'poros' stone—any soft limestone of porous composition used for construction

porphyrytic—(of rocks) dense, igneous, feldspathic rocks of solid colour dotted with tiny flecks

Proconnesian marble—a white marble, veined with grey, quarried on the island of Proconnesus in the Sea of Marmara

propylon—a large entrance gate

sachnisia—the projecting upper portion of a building in wood or lath and plaster, typical of the architecture of Northern Greece and Greek Asia Minor

skene—the stage structure of a theatre

spolia—elements and fragments from ancient buildings re-used in later constructions

stoa—a long, covered colonnade open on one side and closed (by shops or offices) on the other

stele (pl. *stelai*)—a carved tablet, grave-stone or monolithic marker

stylobate—the upper layer of the crepidoma or platform of a temple, supporting its columns *talus*—the outward-sloping face at the base of a solid or fortified wall

telesterion—(from the original building of that name at Eleusis) a large rectangular hall, often with few or no windows, for the receiving of initiates to the 'mystery' cults

temenos—the sacred area surrounding an altar and temple, defined by the peribolos

templon—the masonry structure in a church which closes off the sanctuary

trachyte—a rough-textured volcanic rock with a high content of feldspar

tuff—(Italian, '*tufo*') a stone deriving from compressed volcanic ash: light, porous and resistant

türbe—an Ottoman tomb or mausoleum

INDEX

Nigel McGilchrist is an art historian who has lived in the Mediterranean—Italy, Greece and Turkey—for over 30 years, working for a period for the Italian Ministry of Arts and then for six years as Director of the Anglo-Italian Institute in Rome. He has taught at the University of Rome, for the University of Massachusetts, and was for seven years Dean of European Studies for a consortium of American universities. He lectures widely in art and archaeology at museums and institutions in Europe and the United States, and lives near Orvieto.